TERROR BY RAIL

Conspiracy Theories, 238 Passengers,
and a Bomb Train—the Untold Stories of Amtrak 188

TERROR BY RAIL

THE UNTOLD STORIES OF AMTRAK 188

CONSPIRACY THEORIES, 238 PASSENGERS, AND A BOMB TRAIN

LYNN RADICE

NEW YORK

LONDON • NASHVILLE • MELBOURNE • VANCOUVER

Terror by Rail

Conspiracy Theories, 238 Passengers, and a Bomb Train—the Untold Stories of Amtrak 188

Published in New York, New York, by Morgan James Publishing. Morgan James is a trademark of Morgan James, LLC. www.MorganJamesPublishing.com

The Morgan James Speakers Group can bring authors to your live event. For more information or to book an event visit The Morgan James Speakers Group at www.TheMorganJamesSpeakersGroup.com.

ISBN 9781683506874 paperback
ISBN 9781683506881 eBook
Library of Congress Control Number: 2017911739

Cover Design by:
Rachel Lopez
www.r2cdesign.com

Interior Design by:
Paul Curtis

In an effort to support local communities, raise awareness and funds, Morgan James Publishing donates a percentage of all book sales for the life of each book to Habitat for Humanity Peninsula and Greater Williamsburg.

Get involved today! Visit
www.MorganJamesBuilds.com

Author's Note

This is a true account. I was a passenger on Amtrak 188 when it derailed on May 12, 2015, in Philadelphia. Because of the many people mentioned within these pages, most names and a few of the details have been changed to protect their privacy. Any similarities to living people are merely coincidental and not based on any real connection. Otherwise, the account surrounding the train crash is fact, or opinions, or conjecture related to those facts, based on my own experience and the information made available to me.

Dedication

For my two beautiful daughters, Marilyn and Brigitte, you know the hidden power of divorce, love, loss, forgiveness, and hope. I hope all of these feelings and new inner strength will empower you to be amazing highly successful and happy women. Your Mom Messed Up! I am making up for many lost moments.

For My Mom, Thanks for the catch! Face-planting on concrete hurts!

Brian Daly, AMEN!

For Matisse, without you I would never have written this book or experienced amazing adventures. Some loves burn into your soul. My hope is everyone has many in a lifetime.

To the victims and families of Amtrak 188, may every day be a great new day of hope.

For all my friends at the Academy of Notre Dame de Namur (N.D.A.), it takes a village (and we are one mighty village!).

Deirdre Flint, thanks for reading, for adding great ideas, and for helping me always in life.

Ginny Nagle, thanks for being so sweet and never letting me fail.

Kristen Hubbert, thanks for being my heart and pushing me and listening to me, maybe with earplugs sometimes!

Monica Nask, Terri McClatchy and many many others, thanks for listening and helping.

Dr. Jeanne Lasota, you made high school the best for me.

Dr. Susan Alexander, you are an earth angel!

Bill Noe, David Moore and Bob Compton and Mark and Marc, we are all just pebbles, and never see how we truly affect the lives of others by just a few ideas, positive words, or care. Thank you!

To Jeff, my ex-husband, thanks for being a great dad to your kids!

To all my candidates and clients, LinkedIn friends, new friends, and Facebook friends of many, many years, Thank you! This book is for you and your families. I now know what it means to truly live. There are no guarantees for tomorrow. Stop dreaming of a better yesterday. Love, laugh and live today!

For every single working mom who feels that some days you are too tired or sad to get up, or just feel you can't do it alone anymore: It is not easy! You can do it, and many believe in you! I am one who knows you can! Dig Deeper! Inner strength is a gift.

CONTENTS

Acknowledgement	3
Prologue	5
Chapter 1 Prince Charming	9
Chapter 2 The Parent Swap	17
Chapter 3 Living the Beautiful Life	25
Chapter 4 Brigitte and the Documentary	31
Chapter 5 Meeting a Hollywood Producer	41
Chapter 6 The World at Our Fingertips	47
Chapter 7 Life in the Fast Lane	53
Chapter 8 Off the Rails	59
Chapter 9 Getting Out Alive	63
Chapter 10 Trauma	73
Chapter 11 Recovery is Relative	81
Chapter 12 Train Safety	93
Chapter 13 Bomb Trains	101
Chapter 14 Forever Changed	113
Chapter 15 The Rest of the Story	115
Afterword	119
Appendix 1: News Reports	121
Appendix 2: Survivors Stories	121
Appendix 3: Fatalities	122
Appendix 4: Bomb trains	122
Appendix 5: FBI Warns of Terrorism	122
Appendix 6: Straightening the Curve	122
Photo Journey	125

Acknowledgement

Many thanks to my great readers and editors: Terri McClatchy, Deirdre Flint, and Lana McAra. You were vital to making this happen.

Thanks to the wonderful people at Morgan James Publishing and to Railroad Publishing Company LLC. for a top quality product we can all be proud of.

Prologue

8:56 p.m. May 12, 2015

As my cab approached the curb at Philadelphia's 30th Street Station, I spoke into my cell phone, "Brian Cashman, you can be pain some days, dear. I'm at the train station. I'll email that résumé to you when I get on board." Ending the call, I dropped the phone into my Prada® purse with one hand and swiped my card into the cab's payment machine with the other.

I had less than fifteen minutes to make the 9:10 p.m. train to New York City and no ticket yet. Laptop case over my shoulder, purse on my arm, bulging overnight bag in hand,

I dashed inside. With every stride my black laptop case bumped my hip. I clamped it under my arm to keep it from sliding off my shoulder.

The past week in New York had been hectic, stretching into a long weekend with my two teenage daughters in Philadelphia. I ached with exhaustion. Waiting for a later train wasn't an option. I had to get back to the penthouse on the Upper East Side, crawl into my own bed, and get some sleep. Tomorrow morning would arrive right on time, ready or not.

My back felt itchy. I had on a white sweater covered by a peach Southampton sweatshirt on this 80o evening in May. In those last rushed moments with the girls I had thrown on whatever my hand touched. No time for fashion adjustments now. At least I had on sneakers and not heels.

Inside the station, I headed for the nearest kiosk. My heart thumped in my ears.

I couldn't read the screen and fumbled in my purse for my glasses. 9:03 p.m. Tickets for the 188 still showed up as available. The train was running a few minutes late. Thank God.

Frantically digging in my bag for my credit card, I dropped my wallet. My bags hit the floor when I leaned over to pick it up. *Come on. Come on!*

The printer took forever to spit out the ticket.

Finally, I raced to the boarding platform.

Ahead of me the last few passengers moved into the seven cars of Amtrak 188. A lovely woman wore a playful outfit of orange, red, and yellow. She entered a car toward the back of the train as I hurried toward the front.

I entered the Quiet Car second in line, longingly gazing at those stretched out sleeping. That was not an option for me. I had business to attend to, phone calls to make. No sense wasting the ninety-minute trip with something as indulgent as leaning my head back against the seat and closing my eyes. Constantly on the go with developing a documentary, planning parties filled with high-profile guests by the thousands, writing and speaking, running my highly successful recruiting business—along with my duties as a highly-involved mom—I rarely closed my eyes for anything, and certainly not for a quiet train ride.

The third car still had plenty of room to find a place alone. People talked into cell phones, tapped on keyboards, and played on tablets, totally absorbed without looking up. To all appearances, it was just a typical Tuesday night for travelers headed back to New York City.

About midway back in the car I dropped my things onto a blue seat on the right, my overnight bag on the floor. With a relieved sigh, I sank down next to the wide window, gazing at the reflective darkness outside. Laptop on the tray in front of me, reading glasses ready, cell phone on the seat—I turned on my laptop, ready for work, wishing for a bottle of ice cold water.

I pulled the band from my sagging ponytail and put it back tighter. The password screen appeared on my laptop, and I logged in. As my email came up, I felt a jolt, then another. A shuddering motion shook the car. My glasses hit the floor.

I felt the eerie sensation of a rollercoaster on a downward dive.

A sound like a wind tunnel grew louder and louder. Faster and faster, faster and faster.

Seats rattled. A bag slid off the upper rack and tumbled down the aisle.

Bracing, trying to hold on, I glanced at the woman across from me. Eyes wide, she gripped her seat, lips white with fear. Ahead of me a man shouted, "What the hell?"

A long screech of metal against metal.

The car tilted.

This is how I'm going to die.

Someone screamed.

I think it was me.

Chapter 1

Prince Charming

7:52 p.m. May 12, 2015, Philadelphia

A horn beeped outside the house, letting me know the cab was waiting, meter running.

I was still pulling on jeans and sneakers, scanning the guest room for forgotten items.

I had planned to leave Philadelphia earlier that afternoon, but became engrossed in phone calls and emails. Before I realized it, rush hour had already begun, and it was clear that

I might as well wait until the 9:10 train.

Now the cab was here, and I still wasn't ready.

Carrying my bags, huffing from exertion, I dashed to the street. The moment the cab set off, I reached for my cell phone to text Matisse. He was in Southeast Asia on business.

Two years ago I was a fairly average single mom with two girls, building a life in Philadelphia with my successful recruiting business. That all changed when I met Matisse Marchand.

After dating for a year, I had moved into Matisse's penthouse on the Upper East Side. Now I basked in the brilliant lights and hung out with the beautiful people of New York City—kind of like *My Fair Lady* meets *Pretty Woman*, only classier. Every other weekend, I'd travel to Philadelphia to spend time with my teenage daughters. This was my bi-weekly trek back to New York.

The weekend of my move had started just like this, with a train trip to New York. Matisse was at his company's headquarters in Paris at the time, giving me a chance to unpack before he returned.

As if I needed a lot of time to settle in with my few belongings and Marta, his Haitian maid, helping me. Although she was an excellent cook and diligent housekeeper, I think Matisse's primary reason for hiring Marta was their shared fluency in French. She had been with him for more than twenty years.

I took eight years of French in school. I wasn't quite fluent, but I was learning fast.

Matisse and I had met at the green marble counter of the Carlyle hotel, checking in at the front desk. He stepped aside with that suave European nod to invite me to go first. Tall and fit with thick dark hair dusted with gray, slightly curly in back, he oozed global flair and international charm.

My heart rate picked up. I, the radio personality, suddenly grew tongue-tied and clumsy.

I knocked my credit card to the floor while signing papers. Matisse picked it up. He held it out to me but kept his hold until I looked up, his sparkling brown eyes appreciating me.

He said, "Will you have dinner with me?"

French accent. Wow.

I have no idea what I said to him when I accepted. I was in a trance.

When I reached my hotel room that afternoon, I tore through my bags to find the perfect dress and perfect shoes. I had a long hot soak in the whirlpool tub, then perfect makeup, my long blond hair swept up into a twist with a few wisps hanging down.

Minutes past eight, I entered the wide elevator and closed my eyes to draw in three long deep breaths. I felt a warm glow rise within me. Twenty seconds later I stepped out, poised and radiant in my black strapless gown and four-inch heels.

My sparkling earring caressed my neck when I tilted my head for his soft kiss on my cheek. His *Bleu de Chanel* cologne stays with me to this day.

We sat near the crackling fireplace in the dimly lit room with a candle between us on the round table. He wore a gray Brioni® suit with a dark Hermes® tie and pocket square. We ordered, laughed, and ordered more. Matisse selected wine and had the bottle brought to the table. One sip and I'd never see wine the same again.

Over dessert of milk and honey shortbread and *Chateau d'Yquem*, he leaned forward to say, "I have a place in town, on the Upper East Side. I'm having some remodeling done, so it was easier for me to stay at the hotel tonight. I can't concentrate with the clatter and clutter." He raised his glass toward me. "What a happy coincidence, don't you think?"

We clinked and drank.

Setting down his glass, he smiled. "I hope you will allow me to welcome you there very soon."

"Sounds lovely." I murmured.

When we said good-bye near midnight, he leaned in for another cheek kiss, but I turned my head and tasted his lips. What a night! It was like a fairy tale.

Before I fell asleep, he sent a text, *What a magical evening, darling. Can I see you next weekend? I will be counting the hours.*

Every date he planned a special romantic interlude just for me. He would touch my arm and look into my eyes with his husky voice soft in my ear. He flowed easily from French to Spanish to German or Italian, never missing a beat in that multi-cultural city. His driver would pick me up at the train station in his black Town Car and off we went—to the theater, the symphony, or the opera. Where didn't really matter. It was a dream.

We soon noticed our humor clicked. We liked a lot of same things: travel, caviar, wine, and… anchovies? *Really? You like anchovies?*

Forget it. I was falling fast.

On my first visit to his home two weeks later, I still had no idea who Matisse was in the world. To me, he was a beautiful man with a huge heart and wonderful wise eyes that made me forget my own name.

Fitting his key into the elevator panel, he pushed the button marked P and up we went. He pulled me to him. I felt so safe with my cheek snuggled up to his cashmere sweater.

Stepping out of the elevator into acres of space and mile-deep white carpet, I lost my breath. The art alone… sculptures in lighted alcoves, original oils in wide gilded frames. An artist's dream: spider web encased in a clear box, from twenty sources of spiders, highlighted by a spotlight so each strand glistens.

I'd stepped into another dimension.

In the hallway he had a mosaic of Facebook pictures of couples kissing, hundreds of them in tiny tiles. I caught myself staring, transfixed, before following him into the great room.

He poured wine, and we moved onto the wide terrace. The moon and stars above us, the cityscape stretched out forever. Traffic moved in slow motion far below.

"Do you like old movies?" he asked. I adored the way his cheeks crinkled when he smiled.

"Sure," I said. Had he asked if I liked deep-fried crickets I probably would have given him the same answer.

He put his arm around me. "I've been wanting to watch a certain movie with you. Let's go into the media room."

A few minutes later, we snuggled on the sofa as Carey Grant and Grace Kelly appeared in *To Catch a Thief*. When the movie was over, my head rested against the back of the sofa, so relaxed. He kissed me. Still close to my face he said, "Will you go to the south of France with me?"

I melted into his arms.

After that, I began seeing him often, traveling with him whenever I could. When I had obligations, he would travel with some of his friends. He was very hospitable and had many great friends and family all over the world who welcomed us with warm hospitality. I did not ski much, so sometimes he went skiing with ladies from his business.

In some ways, I felt like I lived a double life. I woke up most mornings in suburbia to tumble out at 5:30 a.m. for a morning jog, waving to the dog walkers, fellow joggers and anyone else who found themselves out at the crack of dawn. After a quick shower, I entered the chaos that is getting two teen girls ready and in the car for school, grocery shopping and other household errands. All of this while taking and making business calls. My Bluetooth headset was my constant companion.

My work-at-home life ran non-stop with cooking, cleaning house, and monitoring homework along with the hundreds of other tasks every single mom does as a matter of course. With three women in the house, the mood swings were the worst. Some weeks I felt like hanging a red dragon on the door with *Enter at your own risk* written underneath.

In the penthouse, calm and quiet reigned. Marta did the cooking and kept the place immaculate. She ran to the store and picked up dry cleaning. If I wanted coffee or tea, all I had to do was ask.

Every other weekend my ex-husband, Jeff, came to visit our two teenage daughters, Marilyn and Brigitte. As soon as Jeff would arrive, I'd head to New York on the first train. Matisse insisted on paying for my trips back and forth and bought an entire second wardrobe for me, so I didn't have to lug too much back and forth, except on certain occasions. While in New York, I wore Chanel®, Armani® and Hermes®. Nothing but the best for me.

At some point in those early months, I learned Matisse was the founder and primary shareholder of a software company in Paris worth billions.

Matisse had a brilliant mind, and I had a voracious desire to learn from him. The more he taught me, the more I yearned to know. We talked of fascinating places, ate amazing food, and drank the finest wines in the world. He belonged to a monthly wine club, so each month he led me through his decision-making of which wines to buy for drinking and which to add to his cellar. Every day was fun and new.

And then the lessons: scuba lessons, golf lessons, tennis lessons. I couldn't get enough.

I wanted to experience everything at once. We hosted parties in New York and exotic foreign locales. We worked and we played—always on the go, always filled with excitement and adventure.

A few months later, we were enjoying a quiet dinner at his penthouse, and I knocked over my glass of *Chateau Lafite Rothschild*. Horrified, I watched that expensive wine form a red puddle on the white carpet. I ran for a towel to clean it up and ducked under the tablecloth for a few moments. When I came up, he had crooked grin and a sparkle in his eye, as though I was up to something naughty under the table. We laughed. I leaned up to kiss him, and we totally forgot about finishing the meal.

With my new connections and growing self-confidence, along with excellent advice from Matisse, I began picking up clients in New York City. My recruiting business took a giant step forward.

Shortly after our one year anniversary, we were in his private jet en route to Vienna for a huge New Year's Eve affair we were hosting there. I would return to New York in five days' time, but Matisse would fly to Belgium and then to Paris for a couple of weeks.

One day, as I was immersed in planning the big event, he suddenly said, "Why don't you move in with me? I want to feel like I'm coming home to you whenever I return to New York."

I slowly took off my reading glasses as I looked up from my laptop. Move in? I had a house in Philadelphia. I had children and responsibilities. Yet at the same time my head was filled with traveling to the best hotels in Thailand, black tie affairs in Cape Town, chateaux in the south of France, Italy, Myanmar, meeting the most glamorous people in the world.

My heart and brain went into a massive tug-of-war. More than anything I wanted to do the right thing—for myself and for my girls.

With my pulse thumping in my ears, I looked into his brown eyes and said, "I'll have to think about that. It would take a lot of planning."

He smiled softly. "You are a master at strategy, Lynn. I know you can do this." He lifted my hand to his lips. "Call me selfish, but I want you with me."

The rest of the weekend my mind stayed in fast-forward, running what-if scenarios. I sank into my seat on the train back to Philadelphia. Who gets handed a choice like this? Love, travel, and a life of adventure. Or playing yo-yo between New York and Philly in some kind of limbo existence. Would I live with the man I love or with my beautiful girls?

That's when it got real. Tears streamed down my cheeks.

What the hell would I tell them… or Jeff?

I remembered the trips we had taken together: Matisse, me, and the girls. They had experienced so much of the world since he came into our lives. I thought of the opportunities that would open for the girls. Also, my business was growing, thanks to many new contacts in New York City. What a chance to expand my endeavors and provide more for them. Maybe moving in with Matisse would be better for all of us.

Chapter 2

The Parent Swap

8:06 p.m. May 12, 2015, Philadelphia

Even at this hour, traffic stayed heavy. On the way to the train station, the cab took Montgomery Avenue past Lasota High School, my girls' school. I hoped they would make lifelong friends like I did.

I met my BFF, Leila, at N.D.A., and we're still like sisters. We were friends all through high school and roommates at Villanova. What stories we could tell! Back then I had a huge fiery mane of curly red hair. I looked like orphan Annie. I switched to long, straight blond after the divorce. Now we even look like sisters

Leila has been through a lot, but she still has such an upbeat spirit. She's the one who gave me a copy of *The Secret*, a book that changed my life.

17

I can still hear her scream when I announced my decision to move into Matisse's penthouse.

We were in Starbucks® with BFF #2, Leslie, the brunette of our trio. Leslie is the sweetest thing ever. She's spirited and fun and an amazing realtor. In all the years we've been friends, I've never heard her say anything bad about anyone. She's been married to her high school sweetheart forever. That's the kind of person she is.

The three of us have been inseparable for more years than I like to count. Age is just a number, right?

We talked for hours about my move to New York. "It would be a win-win-win for everyone involved," I told them. "What I need is a plan to make the change seem natural and easy. I need my girls and Jeff to see the benefits, too."

My daughters, Marilyn and Brigitte, are my life. I hear people say that all the time, but it's true. They put meaning to everything I do. At that time Marilyn was a popular senior in high school, and Brigitte was a bubbly freshman.

Marilyn is gorgeous, with long blond hair and a figure to die for. Always popular, she played field hockey and served on the student council. She worked at a yogurt store and hung out with a great group of friends. Parties and football games were her social life.

I was always jealous that Marilyn was able to get straight A's and manage her social life so well. It was hard to come down on her because she actually got where she wanted to go. She will be successful. She understands people and has a great personality.

At five feet eleven, Brigitte is the tallest by far of the three of us. Already a beautiful girl at fourteen years old, she played volleyball and softball and loved acting in school plays. Brigitte stayed on a constant trek of activities from ice skating, pizza, shopping malls, movies, and stayovers at a friend's house. More often than not, a Friday night sleepover would end with a phone call asking to stay for the whole weekend.

As fun, and outgoing, and smart as her sister, Brigitte just learns differently. She thinks outside the box and comes up with solutions much faster than anyone I know.

Both my daughters have enough spunk and wisdom to set world on fire if they choose to. They have also both been knocked down many times. Each time, their brain rewires, and they get back up to fight again.

Up until that year, Brigitte had attended a small private school for dyslexic children, but at the end of eighth grade, she became obsessed with going to "regular high school" as she put it. The private school didn't have many activities and some of the kids were socially awkward. Brigitte saw Marilyn living the life with clubs and events and tons of friend and that's what Brigitte wanted, and argued and fought until she got it. I knew Brigitte deserved a chance, so I gave in to her.

That's where the problem started.

Marilyn belonged to the "too cool for school" crowd who cut class and hung out on the weekends. She hardly opened her books and flew through high school with A's. Marilyn's friends welcomed Brigitte, and she was thrilled. On the other hand, Brigitte had to study and study hard to pass. She needed focus, but her new social circle did anything but focus.

That also started the "Marilyn says" phase:

"Marilyn says cool kids don't play basketball."

"Marilyn says only weirdos do plays."

"Marilyn says she wouldn't be caught dead wearing pink."

Inspired by Brigitte's school struggles and her unflinching spirit, I was working on a documentary about dyslexia—to highlight hundreds of famous successful people who had dyslexia and the special brilliance they all share. By the time of Matisse's invitation to move in with him, I had about a third of the segments written. Moving to New York would put me near people who could get the documentary into production. So many pluses to making the move.

Sure, we had our share of drama—what family with teenagers doesn't?—but all overlaid with a thick coating of love. Marilyn didn't have to take Brigitte under her wing, but she did. She shared her friends, her activities and her high school wisdom with Brigitte. That is love. For her part, Brigitte loved her sister fiercely and looked up to her in a way that made my heart sing. They weren't just sisters. They were also friends.

The previous Christmas, Marilyn had received a school photo of Brigitte forwarded from a friend. "Look what I just got," she said, holding the iPad toward her sister. "It's you and Jack."

"What?" Brigitte demanded, coming out of her chair. She dropped her cellphone into her jeans pocket and reached for the iPad.

Laughing, Marilyn held it away from her.

That didn't last long. Brigitte was four inches taller than her older sister with longer arms to match. Working nearby at the dining room table, I looked up when I heard Marilyn's wild giggles and Brigitte's shouts of "Give it to me!"

They wrestled and wrangled, four hands on the device. Across the back of the living room sofa, against the wall, they jostled a lamp and knocked over a photo frame.

"Girls!" I shouted, as they swayed near the Christmas tree.

Too late. A huge crash.

The tree limbs bounced after hitting the hardwood floor, tiny glass shards all over the room.

Five seconds of shocked silence.

Brigitte suddenly focused on Marilyn. With a hoot Marilyn dashed for her room where the struggle continued.

Shaking my head, laughing, I pulled the broom and dustpan from the closet. I'd learned long ago that simply cleaning up the mess was far easier than laying blame and putting down edicts. That attitude never worked with my girls.

Minutes later, I passed Marilyn's open door to see them lounging on her bed with the iPad between them, pointing and giggling. I thought about how fun it would be to travel with them at Christmas with Matisse and his children who were always so warm and inviting.

While they were in school I worked mainly from home, but nights and weekends I made phone calls while playing chauffeur and money tree for them.

I loved it, but it was exhausting. Two states and two lives. Now I was about to shake everything up, big time.

I started with a mac-and-cheese dinner. "We're sitting at the table tonight," I said, hands in mitts as I set the casserole on the table.

Marilyn gave me that *something's-up* look and took a seat. Brigitte was on her tablet and didn't notice. I waited until they had their food, ready to dig in.

With repressed excitement in my voice, I said, "I have exciting news." I looked from one to the other, drawing out the suspense.

"What is it, Mom?" Brigitte demanded. She took a bite of mac and cheese. It had crispy breadcrumbs on top, her favorite.

"We're going to Rio!" I cried, hands in the air.

I had expected cheers, but what I got was stares.

Marilyn's chin pulled in. "Rio? As in Brazil?"

I leaned toward her. "In Matisse's private jet to his private mansion on his private beach! After school's out."

The girls looked at each other, mouths open.

Brigitte reached for her phone. "I've got to Google that," she said, sweeping her curly brown hair back from her face, she flicked her finger across the screen lying next to her plate.

"What about clothes?" Marilyn asked.

I grinned. "I guess we're going shopping, aren't we? Let's plan a trip into the City and do it right. We'll start at Bergdorf's."

We spent the rest of the evening talking about the trip and making plans, between the two of them calling friends and spreading the word.

Later, when they were in their rooms with earphones on, I called Jeff, their burly father whose Italian ancestry is discernible in his every feature. Brigitte got her height from him.

Although our marriage had ended five years prior, Jeff remained a devoted dad every step of the way. That soft spot in his heart was the key element to making the housing switch turn out for the best—for the girls, for him, and for me.

I closed the door to my room and spoke into my phone, "I know this is going to sound crazy, but hear me out okay?" Too tense to sit down, I paced from the window to the door.

Silence on the other end of the line. Feeling his instant wariness, I plowed ahead.

"I know you have been saying you miss your girls want to see them more, right?"

"Yes…" His voice sounded doubtful.

I blurted out, "What would you think of buying my house and moving in with the girls?"

"What? Wait a minute," he said. "You're saying you'd move out and I'd move in? Where will you go?"

I told him about Matisse's wanting me to move into the penthouse then rushed on, "The girls will stay here and go on with their lives as usual. We'd switch places. I'll come down every other weekend on the train like you've been doing all these years."

We talked about some details. Finally, he let out a long breath. "I was going to call you," he said finally. "I just landed a job in Philly."

I plopped down on the bed and let myself fall gently on my back. This might just work.

Six weeks later, we made the swap. It went smoothly. The girls were fine with having dad step into the on-site parenting role. They were looking forward to it.

Personally, I had doubts that Jeff would last through the summer with all the chauffeuring and the friend drama and "I need money" requests. Yet it worked. The girls were perfectly content, and Jeff was happier than I'd seen him for a long time.

Best of all, Matisse was kind and generous when it came to my daughters. Our trip to Rio was fourteen days of heaven. He flew down for a long weekend and entertained them with a tour of the city, including a stop at a tiny hideaway restaurant with the best *Picadillo Carioca* I'd ever tasted.

The Rio trip was only the beginning of his generosity. He had the girls bring friends for weekends in the City, a fall trip to Aruba, and on and on. Marilyn and Brigitte were seeing the world, and they were seeing themselves with new eyes. Matisse had two grown children—Elaine and Alain—and they joined us when they could. We had fun. We felt like a family.

Chapter 3

Living the Beautiful Life

8:14 p.m. May 12, 2015, Philadelphia

When my cab reached the Schuylkill Expressway, traffic had backed up to a standstill.

"I'll take Kelly Drive to the train station," the taxi driver said. He was a young guy wearing an Eagles ball cap. "We can keep moving."

I glanced at my phone, still plenty of time to make the 9:10 train.

Moving into the penthouse with Matisse had meant simply bringing the remainder of my spring clothes and setting up my office in a spare bedroom. I rented a storage unit for my winter things and a few mementos. My luggage came with me on the train. I shipped some cartons and that was that.

Unpacking did hit a bit of a snag, though.

Lifting a sundress from the blue suitcase on the bed, Marta said, "This is the last one. We're can't get more in there." Her smooth open face was sober with concern. She stepped into the closet door, still talking. "There is no more room."

"What?" The closet was the size of my bathroom in Philadelphia. Of course there was room. I took a look.

Marta was right. The entire right side had garments in plastic covers with boxes below them.

"What are these?" I asked.

"Those belonged to Jessica," she replied, looking down. "The boss said to leave them."

Jessica was Matisse's wife of over twenty years. She had died of cancer a few years before we met.

I drew in a breath, considering, then decided, *best leave sleeping dogs lie.*

"We'll take the rest to the spare room where I'm setting up my office," I told her, closing the closet door. "I'll organize everything later."

Living in the penthouse had tremendous benefits that freed up my time. Most of all, I was no longer a soccer mom. No more school runs or kid chauffeuring on nights and weekends. Jeff had that covered now.

Marta took over most of the household tasks that had kept me busy in Philadelphia. She was a great cook, always gracious and helpful. She was at our beck and call, and she acted as the butler, too. She scrubbed the kitchen and the bathrooms, and kept the furnishings gleaming. Matisse seemed perfectly content with this arrangement, but I noticed and appreciated everything she did. It was a new way of living for me.

I should have had plenty of free time, but somehow that didn't happen. My recruiting business started picking up with New York clients coming in from our social circles. I made progress writing my dyslexia movie. I started ballroom dancing classes to improve my posture, and I joined several organizations to make more connections.

Near the end of spring, we hosted a gala at a beautiful, world-renowned hotel in Brussels with RSVPs from 450 guests. I negotiated the reservation for the Grand Ballroom of the hotel with a room block that covered three floors. I lined up the live entertainment, the flowers and ice sculptures, I brought in ladies clothed only with body art. Selecting the very finest in food and wine, I worked for weeks planning the event and making the arrangements. I arrived three days early to oversee the details.

The event went off without a hitch. Everyone gushed at how lovely it was. Matisse was beyond thrilled. I was thrilled that Eileen and Alain could make it. I had worried about their flights in from all over.

After that, all party planning fell to me. From Cape Town to Dubai, Shanghai to Copenhagen—We flew. We partied. We schmoozed. We fell into bed at 4:00 a.m. We were back to business by 9:00 the next morning. We were always meeting great friends, and going out to fabulous dinners.

Somehow, I kept my recruiting business in full swing.

Through this time, my father was waiting for a double lung transplant. My father was my best friend. I am a lot like him, a huge giver with a giant heart.

He lived in Pittsburg and I would often take the train to visit him. I told him about my travel adventures with Matisse. Dad enjoyed my stories for hours on end. He had been sick for six years with the ups and downs that go with chronic illness.

He would tell me stories about when he drove an oil truck to make extra money for Christmas as he was often short on funds. When he delivered oil to struggling families and he could tell they were buying heating oil instead of food, he would often stop to pick up a Christmas dinner for them and leave it on their step.

By the time he finished his stories, I was wiping tears and bending over him for a long hug. I loved my dad so much.

Shortly before our trip to Thailand, my dad got his lungs. The surgery went well, and we had hope. However, a few days before the trip I got a call from my Mom. "Your father had complications, Lynn," she said.

I dropped everything to rush to his bedside.

I stayed with him, glad he was surrounded by family. He slowly stopped breathing and passed on. When I realized he was gone, I trembled and sagged against the wall, sobbing.

This was reality. My dad, my source of love, encouragement, and laughter, was gone. Life had changed forever.

My first thought was to postpone our Thailand trip. Matisse flew in and never left my side. He was such a comfort in that difficult time. He was so great with the girls and my mother as well.

He got to meet all my extended family, and my mother immediately took to him, as did my brother Robert. Robert and I have always been close, but we both work long hours, so sometimes it's difficult finding time to visit. Robert works in network news in Philadelphia, and is as smart as he is handsome. *You're welcome, Bro!*

The day after the funeral, Matisse and I left for France, Thailand, and Myanmar.

We flew first class on Thai Phoenix Airline. They served caviar and champagne, with only six seat beds in entire section, complete with silk pillows. Many attendants waited on our every need. I had never seen this type of service or space or elegance on an airline.

How delicious to close my eyes and truly rest. I felt deeply loved, and I knew my dad was looking over me. I had made right decision to go on this journey, which would be a delight-filled, healing adventure.

At 2:45 a.m. after our arrival in Thailand, my hair looked like a snarl of cobwebs held back in a wide clip. Touching up my makeup in the powder room, I cringed at the grief lines so visible in the mirror. My eyes were bloodshot from crying.

Oh well. I hurried to the living room where my laptop waited in a far corner of the Presidential Suite, out of earshot while Matisse slept.

I had a Skype conference call at 3 a.m. local time.

"Brian? Are you there?" I spoke into my laptop, watching the screen, praying the Internet would connect. Even in the finest hotel, connection to the World Wide Web could be spotty in this far corner of the world.

Despite the fuzzy picture and fuzzier sound, Brian's smiling face appeared on the screen. "I'm here, darlin'." Based in Houston, Brian has the good looks of Matt Damon.

Thankfully, the Internet held for the hour we were on, probably because no one else was using it at that insane time.

Conference calls in the middle of the night were only one reason I hardly slept on that trip. After hearing the horror stories of cobras under beds and in closets, I couldn't get the idea of snakes out of my mind. The slightest breeze and I'd come wide awake, my heart thumping.

Shortly before we left Thailand, I took a day off to visit the Wat Phra Kaew temples. I'll never forget the tiled courtyards and the dozens of golden spires. People sat in the open air, some praying, some with cameras. It was like stepping into another dimension—parades of boys with shaved heads and red robes, the markets of colorful fabrics, and buckets of bugs meant for eating.

I enjoyed riding the "tuk tuks", a weird cross between a three-wheeler and a rickshaw. The private outdoor pools and spas were amazing. I took a massage class and learned how to use my thumbs in ways I'd never imagined possible.

Life was incredible. But I hadn't counted on something. The guilt. My girls were doing great living with their dad, so mostly my moods were just a mom thing. I knew that and recited it to myself a hundred times a day. Regardless of that, the guilt of leaving them stayed with me every minute of every day like a dull ache in the back of my mind.

Chapter 4

Brigitte
And the Documentary

8:32 p.m. May 12, 2015, Philadelphia

Traffic on Kelly Drive moved slowly, but at least my cab kept moving. I might make it to the train station yet.

My phone chirped with a text from Matisse. *Be safe, darling. See you next week. Can't wait!*

We had been together two years by the calendar, but he had been away more than half that time. His business demands were great and his social circle was wide. His busy life kept him on the road much of the time. It seemed I was always kissing him good-bye next to a waiting cab.

One notable exception to this was last fall, when I flew to Los Angeles to meet with a Hollywood producer. That time he had been the one kissing me good-bye on the sidewalk. His longtime friends Mary Ann, Susan, Julie and Brittany would be stopping by over the weekend and he would host them on the terrace, so I knew he wouldn't spend the weekend alone.

I remember how good it felt when he squeezed me tightly to him. "Safe trip, darling," he had murmured in my ear.

I clung to him. "Thank you for all you've done to help me get this project off the ground," I said.

He pulled back to look into my eyes. "Call me the moment you're safely on the ground in L.A."

I nodded. A brief kiss, and I hurried into the backseat of the cab. My flight took off from JFK in ninety-two minutes.

That journey had actually begun more than seven years before, when Brigitte was in first grade.

Shortly after school had started that year, I received a yellow slip stapled to her daily papers. *Please call this number to schedule an appointment with a school administrator.*

Under the yellow slip I found an unfinished test paper with Brigitte's baby scrawl on it.

Sweet-faced Brigitte gazed up at me, her gorgeous blue eyes sparkling. "Can I have a juice box?" she asked.

I nodded absently. "Did anything happen at school today?"

She nodded. "We cut circles. Gween ones and wed ones and yellow ones. Then we pasted them to a big stoplight." She headed for the fridge. "Teacher hung them on the wall."

She couldn't get the *r's* no matter how much I tried to coach her. Once at a playdate, her little friend said, "What's your name?"

Brigitte said, "Bweegeete"

"What?"

My little sweetie said it again and again until she finally burst into tears. I stepped in to say it for her, but I felt so bad for her. Imagine not being able to say your own name.

While she found her juice box in the fridge, I frowned at the slip in my hand and picked up my phone to make an appointment with the vice-principal the following morning.

Pencil-thin and precise, Jodie Strauss stayed seated behind her desk when I arrived. Her narrow mouth curved into a tight smile. "Thank you for coming, Mrs. Radice."

That irked me. No one called me *Mrs.* any more. This was the 21st century, after all.

I parked on one of the two chairs facing her metal desk and waited. Whatever it was, I had a sinking feeling the news would be anything but good.

"Last week, Brigitte's class took their standardized tests. Brigitte was unable to complete her test at all."

I nodded. "I saw it in her papers."

Ms. Strauss went on, "I'm sorry to tell you that Brigitte has every earmark of having dyslexia."

My face went numb. "What are you telling me?" I demanded. "Brigitte's not mentally challenged. She's very smart!"

"I know it appears that way," the vice-principal replied, carefully forming each word. "However, I have to inform you that Brigitte doesn't have the capability to meet school standards. You'll do her a service by placing her in a school focused on her learning style and finding a good vocational school when the time comes."

The discussion ended almost before it began. No matter what I knew. The experts were the experts, and I was only a mom. A mom with a bright little girl bursting with creativity, eager for information, and in love with life. Brigitte excelled at things Marilyn and I could never do.

The moment I left the office, the pressure building in my chest almost choked me.

I reached my car and sat there for thirty minutes crying my eyes out. My beautiful brilliant Brigitte had fallen into the machinery of a school system that made zero allowance for kids who didn't fit the norm. It was so unfair.

I put my car key into the ignition, and my mission took shape. I would find a way for Brigitte. Whatever it took, I would find a way.

Within days, I connected with Dr. Susan Alexander, a child psychologist who would provide Brigitte with additional testing.

The moment I entered her office, I felt relieved. Dr. Alexander handed me a chart with practical signs of dyslexia defined. She gave me a moment to look it over.

At that moment, the Einstein Gene Project was born. Imagine if parents, doctors, and teachers had a chart like this as part of a routine yearly checkup. I could have self-diagnosed my child if a chart like this had come my way sooner. I made a mental note to jot some ideas down as soon as I left her office.

When I looked up, Dr. Alexander asked, "How old was Brigitte when she started talking?"

"Almost three. She'd say a few words but no full sentences for a long time."

"What about tying her shoes?"

I smiled. "Her dad has driving himself crazy trying to teach her. I thought she wasn't interested in learning."

Dr. Alexander nodded. "Most parents think their child isn't focused or motivated, but that's not the case. They just don't get it."

She went on, "When these students are identified early on, they can excel. Some pass their peers. When they get lost in the system, they can develop a failure complex. Without support or the appropriate educational methods around them, some may drop out of school, become depressed, or self-medicate. It's such a waste. These students can be helped. Brigitte is one of the lucky ones. She will learn."

During our work together, Dr. Alexander took away the "flaws-and-signs" aspect of dyslexia, the mindset that something's wrong with my kid. She gave us hope and referred us to some excellent schools specifically for kids with non-traditional learning styles. She spoke of the positives and all the famous people with dyslexia. All the possibilities!

I could hardly believe my good luck. Brigitte started second grade in a place that understood her. I was beyond delighted.

Brigitte thrived in the new environment. I knew she would.

A few years later, we were enjoying the slower pace of Christmas break, sitting in the family room watching *Miracle on 34th Street* on a snowy Philadelphia afternoon. Marilyn and Brigitte sprawled on the sofa while I sat in the lounge chair holding my laptop, cruising the Web without any real focus.

In the sidebar on Facebook, I came upon a notice about a documentary contest called "In Search of the Truth." They were looking for true stories of people who were fighting a battle of some sort in their life, stories about their struggling to find solutions to their difficult situations.

I clicked.

Immediately, my imagination started pinging. What a fun mother-daughter bonding project for the holidays. "Hey, let's write a movie!" I called out.

The girls glanced at me, thinking nothing of it. They kept watching their video while

I devoured the information on the website.

We had a true story of what had happened to Brigitte. We could make a documentary about specialized schools for kids with dyslexia. I could be this big mouth for parents like me who don't understand their options. I could be a voice for all the parents who know their child is struggling and failing but have no idea why or how to help them. I was lucky. I tripped over great people and hoped now I could pay it forward.

After their promo video was over, I got up to sit next to Brigitte to show her the website. "Let's see what we can come up with, OK?"

Always eager for a creative project, Brigitte ran for a spiral notebook and a pen.

Over the next two weeks, we put together an outline, lined out some sequences, and wrote some narrative. We had fun. I never dreamed it would go further than that.

Then, we made the first cut.

Wow. On to Step Two.

I met with my high school friend, Jodi McClain, an awesome writer and University of Notre Dame graduate. She spent hours and hours helping me take the project to a whole new level. This was going to happen.

My artist friend Anne Sullivan kept up with how the movie project was going. She kept me motivated with her beautiful enthusiasm. She used to say, "Lynn, you are on your way to being an overnight success."

Friends like these kept me going, and they keep me going to this day.

I put together a promo. I hired a videographer for a day and traveled to D.C. to the mom's group Decoding Dyslexia[1] to record video. Other groups stepped up: the International Dyslexia Association[2], the Yale Center for Dyslexia & Creativity[3] and the Congressional Dyslexia Caucus[4] among them. I researched famous people who have dyslexia and found Richard Branson[5], Keira Knightly[6], Orlando Bloom[7], Tim Tebow[8], and Stephen Spielberg[9]. All of them have spoken publicly about their struggles and triumphs as a result of dyslexia.

I started filming parts of the documentary in Cape Town, South Africa. While there I met a beautiful soul named Benhad, a local advocate for dyslexia who agreed to be in the documentary talking about the Davis Methods[10], an approach to harnessing the powers of a dyslexic mind.

Along the way, people in Greece, Spain, Italy, the U.K., Australia—50 countries in total—wanted to get involved. Momentum kicked in. I started hiring day people for the movie. Matisse was financing some of it, and even came to Cape Town to support me on filming day.

From the first filming, I put together a trailer, a bio about myself and why I wanted to create the documentary entitled "The Child Cage."

We made it through Level Two, Level Three, and all the way to the final cut. We were finalists! This was all above my skillset, so I was reaching out for people to help me, and they showed up at just the right time.

The contest finalists had to appear before the judges' panel and pitch their documentary. My script still wasn't in finished form, but it was as good as I could get it. In true Lynn fashion, on the day of the event I packed up what I had and headed for the studio in the City. I had a date to keep with the judges (all famous, all accomplished in their fields) – no big deal.

1 https://decodingdyslexiava.wordpress.com/
2 https://dyslexiaida.org/
3 http://dyslexia.yale.edu/
4 https://dyslexiacaucus-brownley.house.gov/
5 http://www.businessinsider.com/richard-branson-dyslexia-as-advantage-2015-4
6 https://thepowerofdyslexia.com/keira-knightley-dyslexia/
7 https://thepowerofdyslexia.com/orlando-bloom/
8 https://thepowerofdyslexia.com/tim-tebow-dyslexia/
9 https://thepowerofdyslexia.com/steven-spielberg-dyslexia/
10 https://www.dyslexia.com/research/articles/south-african-researchers/

Signs of Dyslexia in Young Children

Speech Development
- Delayed learning to talk
- Slurred pronunciation
- Difficulty pronouncing long or complicated words,
such as buskettee for spaghetti
- Mixing up names of things, places, and people

Difficulty with Sequences, such as:
- counting
- the alphabet
- telling left from right
- days of the week
- following directions with more than 2 steps

Coordination
- Difficulty clapping to a beat
- Difficulty with directions (up/down, front/back, right/left)
- Switching hands when coloring or drawing
- Difficulty learning to tie shoe laces

Reading & Writing
- Difficulty connecting letters with their sounds
- Difficulty recognizing spoken words that begin with same sounds
- Difficulty recognizing rhyming words
- Difficulty learning to write (writing letters
  or words backward is not a sign until after 1st grade)
- A smart child who has difficulty with reading or spelling

*History: A distant or close family member had difficulty
with reading and spelling*

Chapter 5

Meeting
A Hollywood Producer

When I finally entered the judges' room, I saw the three "In Search of the Truth" producers sitting behind a table in a bare room with a single folding chair front and center for me. Can I say nerve-wracking?

Nothing prepared me for the grilling they gave me. At one point, one of them asked me, "In Scene 7, what do the curtains look like?"

I was a deer in headlights. Who knows what I stuttered and stammered? I certainly don't.

Near the end of the meeting, one judge said, "You might not know that two of us at this table have dyslexia. We learned how to fake it to make it. That's why we are interested in your topic." Frowning, he flipped some pages in front of him. "We're going to ask you to rewrite this. You have potential here. Let's get something decent written, and take it to the big screen."

I left the studio feeling pumped. Not a win this time around, but this idea could actually fly.

I rewrote it.

One in five children has dyslexia at some level. It is genetic. However, few parents realize their student has the condition, so there are few people looking for answers. A parent who suspects their child might have dyslexia faces the dilemma of not wanting to "label" their child versus getting the help they need. And, yes, this is the 21st century.

Since I'm in marketing, I created a marketing campaign featuring the "Einstein gene"—so named because Albert Einstein[11] had dyslexia. I would show dyslexia as a door to genius and make it a good thing.

I could do this.

Shortly afterward, I came across some high-profile people on Facebook. One of them was a movie producer. At first I thought it was a fake account, but when I messaged him, he was, indeed, THE producer he claimed to be. I'll call him Casper Guichard.

I typed into the message box, *Hey, I have this project. Would you take a look at it?*

After a few minutes of discussion, he agreed to meet me at the Four Seasons Hotel in Beverly Hills for dinner two weeks from that date.

This seemed too good to be true. I told myself. *Don't expect too much to happen.* Worst case scenario, I'd have a fun vacation.

---

11 https://thepowerofdyslexia.com/famous-dyslexics/

I arrived at the Four Seasons Hotel, checked into my room to put on my new dress—a hot orange mini with matching four-inch heels—then headed downstairs for hair and makeup. My meeting with Casper would happen in three hours. I had to look the part.

The hotel salon had gold-trimmed everything. A glittering chandelier made the room twinkle.

My stylist was a willowy brunette with flawless skin, long slender hands and a silky French accent. "Please, this way," she said, with a warm smile. "I am Flavia."

I was so nervous and excited that I blurted out, "I'm here to meet a producer to talk about my documentary." My phone stayed glued to my hand. I turned it over to look for a message. I hadn't checked for at least thirty seconds. I told her the entire story of the contest and meeting Casper Guichard on Facebook.

"I'm not sure if he's even going to show up," I said. "I'm a nobody… just a single mom."

As her hands deftly moved, Flavia kept saying, "*C'est bon!* Impressive."

She was about halfway through my down-do when my phone chirped. A text. *Sorry to cancel but it's my son's birthday and I can't get away.*

I lost my breath. How could he do this to me?

"What is it?" Flavia asked.

"I can't believe it." I gasped. "I paid for a flight and a hotel… and it's not going to happen. He just canceled." My voice grew louder. I couldn't help it. "All that money down the drain!"

Flavia's shapely mouth formed an *O*. "Don't you let him get away with that! This is the kind of thing that happens all the time in L.A.

You're a single mom. You came all this way, and you spent a fortune. Convince him, Lynn! Make him see you!"

OMG. She lit a fire under me.

My hands were shaking, but I texted him back. *I'm a single mom, and I came all the way from New York just to see you.*

I paid for a hotel room. You can meet me at my hotel any time, even 3 o'clock in the morning.

I can stop by after your son's asleep or whatever you prefer, even if you're in your jammies.

I do not want to go home without seeing you. You are the sole reason I came out here.

I dropped my phone to my lap and felt like fainting. Flavia brought me a glass of water.

My phone chirped. *I'll meet you tomorrow around lunchtime.*

I sank back in the chair, weak as a kitten.

Flavia gave me a hug, and we laughed. Then I cried. If it hadn't been for her, I would have caught the next flight home, rejected and dejected.

"Tell 'em Flavia Fleitte sent ya!" she said, in a surprisingly dead on impersonation of a Wild West cowpoke.

Feeling like I was sleepwalking, I left the salon and went to the elevators, intending to spend a few minutes in my room then get some dinner. My phone was acting weird, and I was fiddling with it. Still playing with my phone, I got into elevator. It died as the doors closed.

I looked up to see Jennifer Garner, Steve Carell and Bella Thorne in the elevator with me.

I shook my head and said, "This is the worst mommy moment ever. Of course, my phone just died."

In his best *The Office* voice, Steve Carrel says, "No one's going to believe you!"

He was right. My kids were going to think I made it up.

I called them as soon as my phone had enough charge and ended up ordering delivery. My stomach was filled with butterflies. No room for a real meal.

The next morning, I was having breakfast when my elevator buddies came downstairs. They spotted me and came over.

"Got your phone?" Steve asked with a wide grin.

I nodded, grabbing for it on the table next to me.

They posed with me, and I snapped a few selfies. How nice of them! I texted the photos to my girls. This was good karma.

A few minutes before noon, I took the elevator down to the hotel restaurant. A part of me still doubted Casper Guichard would show up. Unfortunately, I looked nothing like I had the day before. I had on a black-and-white dress that was all business. Flavia's handiwork had faded into my pillow, after tossing and turning all night.

The moment I entered, I spotted Casper sitting to the left in the dining room. The booth looked like a high-backed sofa with a chandelier resembling a cloud of bubbles floating overhead.

I'd recognize him anywhere: classic good looks—Yes, my heart raced a bit!—slim face, square forehead and strong jaw. He seemed relaxed, leaning back into the corner looking at his cell phone.

A slim bald server paused by his table to ask, "Can I get you an Americano, Mr. Guichard?" He glanced up and nodded. The server hurried toward the bar.

I politely paused nearby. *This is the real deal, Lynn. This is your chance.*

Catching sight of me, Casper said, "Lynn?" When I nodded, he raised his hand toward the opposite side of the booth.

The moment I sat down, he started laughing. He handed me his cell phone. "Look at the texts you sent me yesterday."

I glanced at it and handed it back. "Yeah?" I didn't get it.

He said, "Now, re-read it."

"What do you mean?"

He read out loud:

"I'm a single mom, and I came all the way from New York just to see you. I paid for a hotel room. You can meet me at my hotel any time, even at 3 o'clock in the morning. I can stop by after your son's asleep or whenever you like, even if you're in your jammies."

I covered my open mouth and cried out, "Oh, my fricking God!" My face was on fire.

He burst out laughing. All my nervous energy let go. I laughed and held my sides and laughed some more.

That broke the ice. Suddenly, we were good friends.

I handed him my script. "This is sort of a *Rudy*-meets-*Philadelphia* global awareness campaign," I said. He leafed through the script as we talked. For the next four hours he wanted to know everything about the project. Because of some recent challenges in his own life, he was looking for a unique project to give back. My dyslexia documentary fit perfectly.

What a random, non-random moment. I'll never forget it.

He ended the meeting with, "Your script still needs work. Find a professional writer and get back to me when you have a decent script."

So I did. I found a writer and commissioned the work. Casper Guichard was waiting.

Chapter 6

The World
At Our Fingertips

8:46 p.m. May 12, 2015, Philadelphia

The cab picked up speed for a few seconds then slowed down again. We were still on Kelly Drive. I speed dialed Brian Cashman for a quick check-in.

"Brian!" I smiled when he picked up. Such a great guy to work with. "Got a minute to talk?" I reached for my notes crammed into the outside pocket of my laptop case. "You're gonna love what I've got for you..."

How different life had been just one year ago. The second week of May, 2014, I paid the cab and let myself into my former home on a Friday afternoon. Jeff was already on his way to northern Pennsylvania to visit friends for the weekend.

Closing the door behind me, I heard a muffled noise coming from the bedroom area and dropped my overnight bag and purse to the carpet.

Seconds later, I found Brigitte face down on her bed, sobbing. She had on jeans and an oversized teal sweatshirt. Her school backpack lay in a heap beside the bed along with a few stray books.

I leaned close to her. "What's the matter, Brigitte?"

She jumped a little, surprised to see me. Rubbing the heels of her hands into her eyes, she sniffed and scooted over so I had room to sit down. Her face was red from crying. "I failed my math test... Again."

My heart sank. "Oh, honey. I'm so sorry." I brushed her curly hair back where it stuck to her cheek.

"I don't know what to do!" she blurted out. "I try and try, but I just can't..." Another bout of sobbing.

I tried to comfort her, but I knew this was the writing on the wall.

Brigitte wasn't great with numbers. Once and only once I let her plug the address for her friend's house into my GPS. She diligently put in the house number, street, and zip code. After a two hour ride we realized something was wrong. I had to pull the car over so I could laugh. So we could all laugh. She had put in the numbers backwards. I hugged her and adjusted the GPS. After that, if she wanted to get a rise out of us when we got into the car, she'd say, "I'll do the GPS!" and everyone would laugh.

Between the social pressure of keeping up with Marilyn's crew and dealing with traditional classroom methods, public school was too much stress for Brigitte. Something had to change. She needed an environment where she could thrive.

Marilyn came in a few hours later, assessed the situation, and grabbed an overnight case. "I'm at Colleen's house for the weekend, Mom," she said, heading out. Poor Marilyn kept a lot in during that time. She was hurting, too, but didn't know how to talk about it. She didn't want to add to the tension, so she avoided the situation, and soon began avoiding us. I wish I had been better equipped to deal with the issues dyslexia created for BOTH my girls.

That weekend Brigitte huddled in her room with her earbuds in, her eyes closed, while I cruised the Internet, researching schools specifically for teens with dyslexia. They were far beyond our meager budget, even splitting the cost with Jeff.

This was hardly the fun weekend that I usually enjoyed with the girls.

Late Monday afternoon, Matisse picked me up at the train station in his new black Bentley®. The moment I closed the car door, he said, "What's happened?"

I glanced at him. "How did you know?"

"You're worried about something. It's written all over your face."

I told him about Brigitte's school problems, ending with, "I've been online searching for a high school for kids with dyslexia. They are so expensive!"

He touched my arm. "There has to be a solution," he said. His voice sounded so comforting. Matisse would know what to do. He always did.

I had barely set down my things on our king-size bed when "Stay" by Jackson Browne came over the sound system. I smiled and headed for the living room where he waited with open arms. Whenever we were traveling, we both always wanted to stay a little longer. "Stay" became Our Song.

When it came over the sound system, no matter where we were we would always stop whatever we were doing and slow dance. No more packing or planning or taking calls, just three minutes of pure heaven.

The music faded. Matisse leaned in for a long slow kiss, the kind that melted me.

"Dinner!" Marta called from the dining room.

Arm in arm, we made our way in that direction.

While Marta served filet mignon and braised potatoes, Matisse poured *Chateau Malescot* wine.

He said, "I know someone who also has a child with Brigitte's challenges. I seem to remember they found a good boarding school for their daughter. I'll look up the information for you in the morning." He handed me my glass.

We clinked glasses and sipped. His brown eyes had a kindness in them that warmed me through and through. I was crazy in love with that man.

The following week, I cobbled together a collection of financial aid and student loans, and a generous gift from my grandmother made up the difference. In late August, Brigitte moved into the boarding school dormitory. She played softball, got involved in the school's theater productions, and her grades immediately came up. That year she went to Italy on a school trip. It was a great decision for everyone.

Marilyn and Brigitte spent Christmas with me traveling in Spain while Matisse traveled to Turkey with his family. It was just the thing the three of us needed, serious bonding time – and the beautiful surroundings were a significant bonus! We toured Barcelona, Madrid, and Malaga— eating at the finest places, seeing history that we'd only read about before.

We stopped at a vendor's market, and a royal blue silk top caught my eye. Perfect color and the cut was made for me. I reached for my purse.

"What are you doing?" Marilyn demanded.

"I'm going to buy this," I said, still digging for my wallet. I always carried a large Prada® purse, always stuffed to overflowing.

"Wait!" she said, stopping me with a firm pressure on my wrist. She turned to the shopkeeper and let off a string of Spanish.

I froze. Suddenly the irony of the situation struck me, and I stifled a giggle. Finally, all those Spanish lessons were going to give me some return on investment.

A few minutes later, Marilyn announced a price just above half the amount I had expected.

When we left the stand, Brigitte gave Marilyn a high five, and we all burst out laughing.

"That was awesome!" Brigitte announced. "I want to do that!"

I nodded encouragingly at Brigitte. Motivating her to study Spanish was an unexpected bonus. I shot Marilyn an atta-girl glance. My girls were growing into beautiful young women. It was a dream vacation.

That magical trip led up to a massive New Year's Eve party that Matisse and I were hosting on the French Riviera. The girls flew back to Philadelphia on December 27, 2014, while I flew to Monte Carlo to oversee the preparations. We had rented most of the Hotel Hermitage for the weekend with 2,750 RSVP's for the event itself. This was my biggest event planning project to date. Matisse kept expanding my boundaries, and somehow I managed to keep up.

We had the magnificent *Salle Belle Époque* ballroom which was red from the marble columns to the drapes and the miles of carpet with spillover room on the Crystal Bar Terrace overlooking the bay. The hotel placed warmers outside to ward off the chilly temperatures.

No chairs, only serving tables along one side and a few high tables for setting down a glass. It was standing room only. People tended to stop in for an hour or two, then move on, so an actual count was difficult. All I know is the space stayed elbow-to-elbow crowded until about 3 a.m.

Matisse and I had the Presidential suite overlooking the Port of Monaco. Standing on the terrace three days after the gala, wrapped in my coat with my nose feeling cold, I truly did wish for a few more days to "Stay." I felt bone weary.

His gentle warmth filled the space behind me as he slid his arms around my middle and pulled me close. I drew in a long breath and leaned my head back against him.

"Time to go," he murmured.

I turned to kiss him. He was on his way to Greece, and I wouldn't see him again for two weeks. That was the way our life went, month after month. In some way fast and in other ways, very, very slow.

If it weren't for Caren, Matisse's administrative chief, we never could have stayed as connected as we did during his constant travels. I am also grateful for call forwarding, since I could never keep track of where he was.

For spring break, Marilyn and I returned to Malaga. Now confident in her skills, she would negotiate with vendors and taxi drivers while I chuckled nearby. She was fierce.

We went to the villages of Rhonda and then took a boat across to Morocco where the food was incredible.

Meanwhile, my life in New York continued to expand. While Matisse traveled I was making friends and developing connections. Every week had its classes, events, and meetings. New York is called "The City That Never Sleeps" for a reason.

Chapter 7

Life in the Fast Lane

8:52 p.m. May 12, 2015, Philadelphia

When I saw signs for Drexel University, I knew we were getting close to the train station.

I told Brian, "We're almost there. I gotta go…"

"One more thing," he said, urgency in his voice.

I glanced at the time.

I had expected that moving to New York would slow my life down, but the penthouse had turned into a revolving door of frantic activity.

Matisse came to New York and flew out at odd times. Sometimes weeks would go by without seeing him. Other times he'd be around for ten days, wanting my attention. I never found balance and routine.

I would open wine at 4:00, light candles at 5:00, and music on by 5:30. I'd put away most of my work, so he came home to a peace-filled environment. I read that once in a book about the 1950s. He treated me like a princess, and I treated him like a king. I was grateful for how much my life had changed. This was my way of showing him.

When he'd fall asleep in his chair, I'd cover him with a blanket to let him sleep. I'd always make his coffee in the morning, warming up the milk the way he liked it. I'd mix his yogurt with just the right amounts of plain and fruit, adding specific amounts of grapefruit oils. Matisse was into handball, swimming, and yachting. Fitness was important to him, so he was specific with his diet. I loved taking care of him.

I loved giving massages for no reason. The whole enchilada, complete with oils, hot towels, and candles. A neck massage on long car rides to the Hamptons or just scratching his back or head. I loved sitting in silence listening to his wide range of musical choices—opera, theater, pop, classic, whatever. These precious moments were becoming harder and harder to come by, though.

I now had clients all over the world. My phone became a 24/7 extension of my arm, since I was taking calls in the early hours of the morning to allow for time-zone differences. It wasn't unusual to have an appointment at 2 a.m. that kept me awake for an hour, then I'd have trouble getting back to sleep.

One mega-party could keep me busy for months with dozens of overseas phone calls and thousands of details to manage long distance. Matisse hosted two or three big events a year with several smaller affairs between. What had started out as a fun venture swelled into a monster that gobbled up time I needed for my business obligations.

My recruiting business paid my bills. Party planning brought in lots of love and appreciation, but everyone knows you can't live on love, right?

I got an idea for a recruiting app and put together some plans and a strategy for bringing that to market. I wrote fourteen mini-books on job hunting and interviewing.

Add the documentary into the mix and things started roaring out of control. My nerves stayed tight with the persistent feeling that I was forgetting something. Even when I could find a few minutes to relax, I stayed tense because my mind refused to shut down.

On May 7, 2015, after a beautiful steak dinner with Matisse, I retired to my office while he took a business call.

An hour later, he came to my door. "Are you going to be a while?" he asked. He had the last remaining sip of wine in his glass. "I'm still feeling jet lagged. I'm going to turn in."

"I'll be there in a few minutes," I said, looking his way, my fingers still typing. "I have to get these emails out before morning."

He sighed, paused a moment, and went quietly away.

I glanced at the door, registered that he had left, and continued working. Before I knew it, the clock on the bottom corner of my screen said 1:00 a.m. I yawned and pushed my chair away from my desk.

I had three appointments in the morning before I'd catch the train to Philadelphia for a long weekend with the girls. My contacts in Philadelphia stayed hot because I extended my weekends into Friday and Monday. This week I planned to stay until Tuesday afternoon, May 12. I needed to be back in New York for a medical procedure the next morning, May 13.

While in Philadelphia I always morphed into a chauffeur and an ATM machine. My mini-van stayed in Philadelphia for that very reason. That parking and driving in New York was an expensive nightmare was a factor as well. I'd pick up the girls after school on Fridays, hit the ATM, then distribute cash. Final step: deliver them to sundry destinations – school games, dances, friends' or boyfriend's houses, and countless others.

I'd see them off, then pull into a parking lot and make phone calls or meet Leila and Leslie somewhere fun until time to pick them up.

This particular weekend, both girls were headed to the mall for shopping and hanging out with friends. I popped in to find some casual outfits for a trip to Portofino where Matisse was hosting a gala in six short weeks. Keeping up with Matisse's elegant friends put a strain on my credit cards. It was also fun surprising him with new La Perla® lingerie. I figured high fashion was part of the package and kept swiping, another reason to keep my recruiting business at top performance.

House-swapping with my ex created issues I never expected. The house was the same, but life there looked nothing like it had before. During my visits, I'd crash in the guest room, which was every bit as awkward as you might expect. I didn't feel right leaving any of my things there, so I lived out of a suitcase. We got divorced because we didn't get along, and now we were forced into the same space on a regular basis. It was working, but just barely.

Imagine my dismay at arriving at *my* house (despite everything, I still thought of it in that way) and finding the door to the dishwasher standing open because they were using the clean dishes right out of the machine. The laundry room… Let's just say, it was not a happy time. I had learned to look the other way, because it seemed to be working for the household.

We had totally opposite parenting styles. The kids now lived by different rules. Some were stricter (as in anything to do with boys) and some more lax (as in chores and activities).

I always kept the girls busy with karate, swimming, competitive sports, and other activities. Jeff's philosophy was more open. He was a better friend to them, the fun parent.

I had to simply accept the fact that Jeff didn't do things the way I always had, but he was a great father and had a lot of fun with the girls. He could have used a maid, but the girls were happy. That's what counted.

On Tuesday morning, May 12, I saw Marilyn off to school and Brigitte to her friend's house. We said our goodbyes, thinking that I would be on the train before they got home. However, the day didn't go as planned. I got caught up in culling through résumés and making calls. I might have wandered into the kitchen for a yogurt, but other than that it was work, work, and more work. I was still in my sleep pants and a t-shirt when I heard the front door open.

Seconds later, Brigitte, back from her friend's house, poked her face around the door frame. "You're still here, Mom?" she asked.

"Oh my God. I lost track of the time!"

Brigitte parked on the bed. "I can't believe how much work I have to get done before next week. Some spring break…" She launched into a detailed account of high school kid drama.

I nodded and responded, but my mind was on my failed plans to get out of Philadelphia at a decent hour. I had to report to the medical facility in New York at 7 a.m. for a procedure. I'd planned on having an early night. No point dashing out now only to land smack in the middle of rush-hour traffic.

Marilyn arrived a few minutes later. So did Jeff. The moment he saw me, his face changed expressions. Not negative exactly, just deadpan. God, I hated the awkwardness.

I made a few last PR calls and held an impromptu interview prep with a business analyst from the Upper West Side. Jeff called out for pizza. I took bites while throwing things into my overnight case, completely forgetting to keep out something presentable to wear on the train.

By the time I realized what had happened, I had no time left to pull anything out of the bag. I grabbed a sleeveless white sweater and jeans, then covered them with a peach Southampton sweatshirt. Stuffing shoes into the side of the bag, I slid my feet into white Keds® and pulled my hair back into a ponytail.

A beep outside.

"He's here, Mom," Brigitte said, picking up my laptop case. "I'll take this one for you."

"Thanks, honey," I said, grabbing straps—my purse, overnight case—checking around for anything forgotten. There was always something. Marilyn stepped into the hallway for a quick hug as I dashed by, then they both followed to help me into the cab. I wished for the millionth time that I had more time to spend with my girls.

The moment I reached the porch, the heat hit me. It must be eighty degrees. I had on both a sweater and a sweatshirt. What was I thinking?

"Please, hurry," I told the young driver as he put my bag into the trunk. He was my height and wore a ball cap. "My train leaves at 9:10."

"I will do my best," he said. "It will be close."

What an exhausting five-day weekend. I couldn't imagine showing up for a medical procedure so early the next morning.

Chapter 8

Off the Rails

8:56 p.m. May 12, 2015, Philadelphia

As my cab approached the curb in front of the wide columns of Philadelphia's 30th Street Station, I spoke into my cell phone. "Brian Cashman, you can be a pain some days, dear... I'm at the train station. I'll email that résumé to you when I get on board." Ending the call, I dropped the phone into my Prada® purse with one hand and swiped my card into the cab's payment machine with the other.

I had less than fifteen minutes to make the 9:10 p.m. train to New York City and no ticket yet. Laptop case over my shoulder, purse on my arm, bulging overnight bag in hand,

I dashed inside. With every stride my black laptop case bumped my hip. I clamped it under my arm to keep it from sliding off my shoulder.

Waiting for the later train wasn't an option. I had to get home to my own bed. My medical procedure would happen in less than ten hours.

My back felt itchy, reminding me how overdressed I was. At least I had on sneakers and not heels, so I could run. Inside the station, I dashed past the wooden benches, ignored the ticket windows and headed for the nearest blue kiosk. My heart thumped in my ears.

Just as I reached the kiosk, a young woman with long dark hair and silver dangling earrings grabbed her ticket from the kiosk and strode away.

I couldn't read the kiosk screen and fumbled in my purse for my glasses. Tickets for the 188 still showed up as available. The train was running three minutes late. Thank God.

With scrambling fingers digging for my credit card, I dropped my wallet. My bags hit the floor when I leaned over to pick it up. *Come on. Come on!*

The printer took forever to spit out the ticket.

The time above the notice board said 9:08. I raced for Stairs 5 to the boarding platform.

As I reached the platform, a lovely woman came into view. She wore a playful outfit of orange, red, and yellow. She entered a car toward the back of the train as I hurried toward the front. Ahead of me the last few passengers moved into the seven cars of Amtrak 188.

I entered the Quiet Car second in line. Just inside the door to the left, a red-haired man with a short military-style haircut leaned back in the corner with his eyes closed. He looked exhausted. Several people appeared to be sleeping.

I remembered the phone calls that I needed to make. No sense wasting the entire trip with something as prosaic as leaning my head back against the seat and closing my eyes.

I had far too much to do. I turned around.

The third car still had plenty of room to find two empty seats. I needed to unload my laptop case onto the seat next to me, so I could work. Several people tapped on keyboards with the focus of those who have a lot on their plate. Others talked on cell phones and played on tablets. Everyone was totally absorbed. No one looked up.

A typical Tuesday night headed back to New York City.

About halfway back in the car I dropped my things onto a blue seat on the right, my overnight bag on the floor.

A couple of rows behind me, a young Navy serviceman wearing summer whites sat next to a curly-haired woman with a friendly smile. They were two strangers exchanging pleasantries. Both had their trays down, laptops open.

With a relieved sigh, I sank down next to the wide window, with reflective darkness outside. With my laptop on the tray in front of me, reading glasses ready, cell phone on the seat—I turned on my laptop, ready for work, wishing for a bottle of ice cold water.

I pulled the band from my sagging ponytail and put it back tighter. The password screen appeared on my laptop. I logged in. As my email came up, I felt the car jolt, then another jolt. My glasses hit the floor.

I felt the eerie sensation of a rollercoaster taking flight on the downward dive.

A sound like a tornado grew louder and louder. Faster and faster, faster and faster.

Seats rattled. A bag slid off the upper rack.

Bracing, I tried to hold on. Across from me I recognized the dark-haired woman with large silver earrings from the kiosk. She gripped her seat, white to the lips.

Ahead of me a man shouted, "What the hell?"

A long screech of metal against metal, then intense shaking and the car felt as though it went airborne.

The car tilted right, and I slammed into the window.

This is how I'm going to die.

Someone screamed. I think it was me.

Clichéd as it may seem, my life flashed before my eyes, though not in the way I always thought it would happen. I didn't see my sixth birthday, my high school graduation, or even my wedding day. I saw only those snippets of my life that that coalesced into my being on that very train, in that very car, at that very minute.

I saw Matisse. Our first kiss. Thailand. The Hamptons.
I saw my Jeff moving back into my house.
I saw Marilyn haggling with vendors in fluent Spanish.
I saw Brigitte, dropping her off at boarding school.
I saw myself. Working. Networking. Parenting.
Rushing. Rushing. Always rushing.

Chapter 9

Getting Out Alive

On my back, I opened my eyes to total darkness, inhaling a thick cloud of soot and dirt straight into my lungs. I heard moans and cries for help around me, but had no idea where they were coming from. I didn't even know where I was. I crunched down on hard jagged bits in my mouth.

My hands were crossed in an X over my face, and my arms pressed into something hard. The luggage rack. Suitcases and debris weighted down my legs. I couldn't stop coughing and gagging. My chest ached. My arms felt horribly bruised, and the back of my head throbbed.

I'm alive. I think.

My eyelids felt like sandpaper scraping my eyes. I thought, *My teeth are broken.* I slowly lifted one hand and pulled chunks from my mouth. Silently weeping, I peered into my hand, trying to see. *Thank God! Not my teeth!* My mouth was full of gravel and soot.

Turning my head to spit it out, I felt a stab of sheer agony pulse through my shoulder and my head. I must have slammed hard.

What had happened?

I had been sitting on the right side of the train. That side was now in the dirt, and the left side of the train loomed far above me. I sat up and began to push away the luggage that pinned me down. I sensed the scuffling of others beginning to move about. Tiny lights appeared, cell phones switched to flashlight mode.

A woman hobbled past me in a cloud of black dust, murmuring, "We have to find the exit." She returned a moment later, saying "Where is the exit?"

I felt the crushing weight of claustrophobia for the first time in my life. Darkness inside the train and outside. No emergency lights, no glow-in-the-dark tape to show a path to safety. *I'm trapped in a black box.* Panic pressed my aching chest. I began to hyperventilate, further straining my clogged lungs.

Voices came from all directions. My heart was beating faster, but I tried to calm down and get my bearings. *I'm trapped in a black box. No way out.*

Two male voices sounded close by.

"The doors won't open. Sealed shut! Anyone know how to open them?"

"Pull on them!"

"Doesn't work..."

"Then try pushing them!"

I'm trapped in a black box. I can't breathe. Hurry! Hurry! I'm trapped in a black box.

"No go. Do they seal on impact? Is this for real? Is there a latch, a handle, ANYTHING to get them open?"

"Wait! I think the windows are emergency exits. They might be the only way out."

"The only windows are straight up. How are we supposed to get to them?"

"We'll have to climb the seats."

"How in the hell do we do that? There's nothing to grab onto."

Another voice echoes from a distance.

"Everybody, over here! I see an exit window! We have to pull the rubber from the edges."

More lights began to flicker like fireflies. I was able make out the men gathered under the window.

A woman wandered past me in a daze. "Somebody's trapped in the bathroom," she murmured. She might have been speaking about the weather. Everybody was zombie-like.

I smelled oil... And SMOKE!

I'm trapped in a black box that's about to explode. We have to get out now!

My crew instincts finally kicked in. When on my rowing crew, I learned that when you are sure you don't have anything left to give, you dig harder and grind it out.

This was that moment. Heart pounding, gasping for air. Thinking. And over-thinking.

Time to get out! Somebody pick up the pace before we're all blown to bits.

I shakily stood, hoping my legs could support my weight. My shoulder hung strangely, pulsing pain with every heartbeat. I felt a weird mixture of numbness and overwhelming pain. I was missing a shoe and surrounded by jagged shards of glass. I was terrified to put my bare foot down, but I knew I had to do it.

I limped to where I thought the window was, and said to one of the men, "I'm light. I can get up there if you help me. I can get that window open. Let's do this!"

"Are you sure?" he asked me.

I wasn't, but looking around I saw a woman with blood coursing down her face from a head wound. Another woman stood with an obviously broken arm, hanging down like she had a second wrist. Seats and luggage were strewn like children's toys. A sobbing woman was pinioned under a pile of debris, and a man spoke to her in soothing tones as he tried to free her. Across the car, a man and woman pounded on the door, screaming hoarsely. To my right, a mound of luggage had somebody crushed beneath it.

"If you can boost me, I can do it."

The man cradled his hands to give me a boost, and groaned as my weight settled on him. "You're hurt," I exclaimed.

"Today," he said through gritted teeth, "it's all relative. On three, push up with your other leg." He boosted me up.

Getting up to the window was only the first hurdle. I somehow had to manage to cling to the upended seat with my knees and pull on the rubber around the window. It tore free inch by inch. Finally, I was able to punch the window out of the way. I learned something new that day: how to open a train window. It wasn't easy!

Smoke was filling up the car. Someone bellowed, "Stop looking for your luggage and get out, before we all die!"

I took in a deep gulp of fresh air and felt relief for a moment, but the job was not finished. I needed to get myself up and out of the window. With my shoulder so severely damaged, I didn't know if I could. I took a deep breath and heaved. It was like doing a pull up and then pushing up on parallel bars, all with a broken shoulder, but my body held, and with a final thrust of my arms, I rolled out onto the roof.

No, not the roof – the side of the train! As I lay there, catching my breath, I was surrounded by darkness and silence. Utter darkness. Eerie silence.

Strangely, the atmosphere inside the train suddenly calmed, terror held at bay by that one open window. As hurt and traumatized as we all were, I didn't see anyone panic, putting other people in jeopardy in their quest to get to safety. Instead, people helped each other— guiding the injured toward the way out, offering encouragement, doing whatever they could.

My mind had trouble comprehending the magnitude of the destruction. There was no time to think. We needed to get away from the train.

I spotted a line of people on a hill just beyond the tracks, screaming and pointing. Finally, their words registered.

"Fire! The train's on fire!"

I screamed through the window to the people beneath, "The train is on fire! We have to move NOW!" The level of panic ratcheted back up, and the cries became louder, more desperate.

The man who had boosted me up started to send a steady stream of victims up to me in the same way. I stooped to grab their hands and hoist them through the opening, half in and half out of the window. My strength was crazy. Nothing else mattered. I stooped and lifted, then lifted again. I am not sure how many people passed between me and the Good Samaritan below, but eventually the line stopped.

I hesitated, wondering what was happening. Although the break was a blessed relief, my heart wrenched at the thought of more people trapped below. My broken, battered body had reached its limit. I could do no more.

The man beneath me shouted up, "They've got the back window open! More people can get out that way. It's easier to get to!"

I knew there were more people who needed help, but I turned away. I had my girls to think of. I didn't want them to lose their mother, and I didn't want to die. I took a last look down at the hero who had helped so many. He didn't ask me to help him out. He turned and went back to continue rendering aid.

Tears streamed down my face. My heart was broken, and my mind shut down.

I walked away, and that's a decision I live with to this day. In every waking moment. In every nightmare. I chose to live, for my girls.

I don't know if he ever made it out: that man who helped so selflessly.

I took stock of my position for the first time. Yards away, I saw the mangled wreck that was once Car One, smoke rising from it in waves. Even worse, I saw that Car Two was split in half by a light pole.[12]

I almost sat in that car. Would I be dead now if I had?

I looked out upon an alien landscape. Electric sparks shot into the sky. Smoke filled the air and voices screamed in the distance. It was like a vision from Hell. I felt complete isolation. I was utterly, completely alone as I gazed upon the landscape. Suddenly, my eyes picked out a line of oil tankers on a parallel track, mere yards from my smoky perch. If the fire reached those tankers, we were all doomed.

Fear brought me to action. I needed to get off the top of the train and as far away as possible. Looking over the edge, it was clear to me that my only option was to jump. The ground seemed impossibly far away, though, and I feared that I would be jumping to my death. It was a tragic choice: *Jump and maybe die, or stay and certainly die.*

I jumped.

I have no clue how my broken body survived the jump, but soon I was on the ground, amid tangled metal and warped train tracks. *Are any of the rails "live"?* I thought. *How do train tracks work?* I concentrated on putting one foot in front of the other: bare foot-shoe, bare foot-shoe.

I looked up as a man appeared at the top of the car. He called to me, "How do I get down?" I guess he expected a safe way down somewhere.

12 http://www.fireengineering.com/articles/print/volume-168/issue-10/features/amtrak-derailment-operations-the-first-24-minutes.html

I said, "It's gonna hurt," and stepped away, so he wouldn't land on me.

I had gone only a few steps when I came upon a woman lying on the ground, overcome by her injuries. I peeled off my sweatshirt, excruciating pain making me cry out with every movement. I rolled the sweatshirt into a ball and carefully wedged it under the woman's head. It was a small thing, but I had to do something to ease her misery. I continued trudging ahead, my bare foot encountering broken glass, shards of metal and splinters with every step.

I saw others doing the same. Like a scene out a movie, the end of the world with the walking dead. Everything was in slow motion. Nobody was there to help us. No helicopters, no ambulances. Even though we could see each other, we were all solitary in our silent march.

All alone. All injured.

It looked like death. It smelled like oil and death. And silence, where you aren't sure if it's real or a dream.

A man asked me to help him bind up his two fingers with his tie. They were hanging on by strands of sinew. As I helped him, I was afraid they would come off right in my hand.

Another man had blood gushing from his eye. He said, "How bad am I?"

I couldn't answer. All I could do was cry. He said, "Are you okay?" with concern for me despite his own injury.

Even more horrifying was the sight of those oil tankers just feet away. As I passed them, a man said, "If these tankers had blown, we'd be in a crater right now."

I caught my breath and backed away. It was too much.

Everywhere I looked I saw battered faces and drooping limbs, then stretchers carrying bloody broken bodies. Horrible. Horrible.

A kindly voice brought me out of my stupor. "Let me help you," he said. "I'm a medical student." He touched my good arm. "Come this way."

His voice brought up a choking sob from deep inside me. The pain. The pain. I felt like

I was being torn apart.

He led me to a group of bleeding broken people who could stand up—the walking wounded. With mile after mile of chain link fence surrounding the rail yard, emergency vehicles had difficulty gaining access to the crash site. Anyone ambulatory had to walk out. Most were barefoot. I was pathetically grateful that I had at least one shoe. We had to walk hundreds of yards over broken glass, gravel, and rough wooden rail ties to reach the medical vans.

More than fifty of us waited in a group as van after van transported people to the hospital. They looked like airport shuttle buses. No medical attention, just a ride.

A girl who couldn't have been more than twenty passed her phone around, so people could call their loved ones. I looked at her unmarked face and wondered how she had managed to come out so well and with her phone and briefcase intact. Not a scratch.

When the phone reached me, I called Marilyn. The moment I heard her voice I started crying so hard I could hardly talk. "I was in a train accident," I gasped.

"What??" she cried.

"I was in an accident. My train crashed. We flipped."

A spasm took my breath for a moment.

"Mom?? MOM!!" she cried, voice cracking.

"I'm hurt but I'm okay," I ground out, trying to hold back the pain from my voice. "I'll call you from the hospital. Watch the TV."

"I love you!" Marilyn said. Before the connection cut off, I heard her scream, "Brigitte! Come here!"

Tears oozed down my face. What if I hadn't survived? What would have happened to my precious girls? I had just been lamenting that I didn't have enough time with them, and now I had almost been taken away from them forever.

Finally, it was our turn to get on a van. Next to me sat the young woman who had shared her phone. No one in the van attempted conversation. We were too hurt for small talk. Our only thought was getting help. But when we arrived at the hospital, a man in a white coat opened the passenger door to say this hospital had no room. We had to go to Philadelphia University Hospital in Center City.

Gasps and groans came from the group. Two people started to sob. Would this gruesome nightmare ever end? With more than 200 people in need of medical attention, every hospital in the area was flooded.

Yes, the medical triage rating might say your injuries aren't life threatening, and you can wait to be seen, yet to someone with a shoulder pulsing waves of agony, a foot sliced to ribbons and other injuries, that rating doesn't mean much. Every second seems an eternity.

And yet despite the indescribable pain, I felt lucky. I was alive.

Chapter 10

Trauma

What a relief to reach the Emergency Room. They gave me a wheelchair, and I knew they would take care of everything.

My new friend with the cell phone hung with me. She looked so clean, so perfect. At one point I looked her over and said, "Were you really on the train? Are you sure you're not a journalist trying to get a scoop on the accident?" Normally, I would never be so accusatory, but these were far from normal circumstances.

She gave me a disbelieving look. "Have I been taking pictures and interviewing people? Come on!" She went on, "I was in the last car. We got a bad jolt, but nothing like you did." She scanned me as though taking inventory.

"How do I look?" I asked, touching my face. "Is it really bad?"

She said, "You look like hell." She took my picture.

When she showed it to me I grabbed the phone from her, shocked. My eyes formed two white spots in the middle of my soot-blackened face. My hair looked singed. Blood smears covered my right shoulder. That shoulder hung down in an odd way.

I didn't recognize myself.

After a while, a nurse came around to record my name and contact information. She took my vitals and made notes on my injuries. A female police officer arrived to take our statements about the crash—especially the sounds and sensations we felt before impact.

After a seeming eternity, an orderly came to move me into the treatment area only to leave me sitting in the hallway for another hour. The narrow hallway with patches of blue on the floor took me back to the trapped feeling of being in the train. My eyes swam with tears, and I twitched with the horror of it all. Every jostle of the wheelchair brought a firestorm of pain and a wave of terror. Being here and in pain brought up flashbacks to my two car accidents—one where my car exploded, and the other, a crash in my college days. Comparatively, they were the proverbial walk in the park.

Finally, they moved me to a curtained room and gave me morphine. Blessed morphine.

It was near 1 a.m. by this point. Using the room phone, I called Marilyn to give her an update and ask her to contact Matisse. Then I called my Mom who knew nothing about the crash yet. She promised to call my brother, Robert.

Excruciating x-rays where I had to turn and my shoulder stabbed with pain.

Then an MRI. The machine sounded like a roar in my throbbing head. The tunnel was so tight. No light. *I'm trapped in a black box.* I started sweating. No air. *I'm trapped in a black box.*

I started shaking. Silent tears ran toward my ears. I'm trapped in a black box.

Finally the tech pulled me out and saw I was crying. He said, "Are you ok?"

"I'm not," I said. "I'm not okay."

He helped me off the table and back into my wheelchair for more waiting.

The ER team treated me for soot inhalation and told me my shoulder blade had broken in two. I would find out later that only one percent of impact injuries have a force strong enough to result in a broken shoulder blade. Usually resulting from motorcycle accidents, this level of injury is often accompanied by a broken spine, internal injuries, and spinal cord damage.

What did I get? I got a sling and pain meds along with a release form.

Are you kidding me? They weren't going to keep me as much pain as I'm in?

With growing hopelessness, I signed the paper. Every step of the way things only got worse.

At 3 a.m. the hospital ER staff showed me the door. I called a cab for the hour ride back to my house… or I should say my former house where my ex-husband now lived?

Nothing can describe how alone I felt getting into that cab, dreading the ride and dreading my return to the very house I had left seven hours before—only now I had nothing but the grimy, tattered clothes on my back. I had nowhere else to go. This was not going to be good.

Nothing prepared me for the change in myself when I arrived at the house. Marilyn and Brigitte were waiting, crying and distraught, along with their father. They wanted me to sit with them and tell them what had happened. It was now past four o'clock in the morning, and I was at the end of my endurance. I could only sob and shake uncontrollably. I couldn't talk. I assumed this was from the pain and fatigue of the accident, but when my mother came over the next day, I had the same reaction.

My mind shut down. I couldn't talk about what happened. Not then. Not the next week. Not the next month. Everywhere I went, people swarmed me, wanting to know what happened. I'd burst into tears and turn away. I couldn't.

When I finally made it into the shower, black swirls formed around the drain along with handfuls of hair. I touched the back of my head to feel a massive lump and bare skin. My shoulder hurt so badly, I hadn't realized my head was also bruised. *How in the hell did they justify sending me home??*

The next day, the ER nurse called Jeff's landline number and asked for me. "Hi Lynn," she said. "I had a doctor look over your tests this morning. We need you to come back in for more tests. It looks like you have damage in your neck and back."

What? I swallowed hard, so I could answer her. "Come to the ER again, you mean?"

"Yes. Ask for me at the front desk, and I'll come out for you."

I put down the phone and felt a weird mixture of relief and anger. They had sent me home with nothing but a sling. Who knows what kind of damage had been done? On the other hand, I thank God for a nurse who cared enough to follow up.

This time when I got into the cab, every tiny bump and sway of the car felt as if the car were careening out of control. I couldn't hold back the panic. "Don't go so fast!" I cried to the driver. At every turn I knew the car was about to flip over. "Watch out!" I lay down on the seat because I couldn't stand to see the scenery passing by. Was I losing my mind? I was certain that I was losing my mind.

More tests, more orthopedic support, and more medication—that's what my trip did for me along with another expensive cab ride home.

Everyone at the house stayed glued to the news coverage of the train crash. They were obsessed with it. I wanted to get away from the memory, but they had the news on all over the house.

Two days after the accident, I had to get some clothes. Mine were forever lost in the crash debris, and I never left any personal items in Jeff's spare room. Another lonely cab, a pain-riddled hour finding something that would be easy to get on and off, and agonizing moments in the fitting room.

The financial burden of all this pressed on me. The loneliness pressed on me. I had always been successful and in control. I didn't want the girls to see me fall apart. I was too proud.

These are the practical realities of accident victims. The simplest tasks become a monumental chore, and many of them were impossible—such as washing the left side of my body, lifting a purse or jug of milk, even combing my hair. Unrelenting PTSD and brain fog swept in as well.

At the entrance to the fitting room, the silver-haired grandmotherly woman working the desk noticed my distress. "Do you need help?" she asked. "You look like you're in pain."

"I was in the train accident," I blurted out.

She stared into my eyes. "THAT accident?" she gasped. "Oh My GOD!"

My heart lurched. I backed away from her. Somehow I made it through the fitting room alone.

I decided to stay in Philadelphia for a few weeks. Perhaps more honestly, the decision was made for me. My medical insurance was still in Pennsylvania, and I had to make the round of doctors, start rehab, and begin psychiatrist visits for severe PTSD. More tests showed permanent damage to my neck and back. I was left with restricted range of motion and pain that never ceases. My memory, multi-tasking, and sense of humor went into hiding, pinned down by dense brain fog.

I took to wearing soft hats to cover the three-inch bald spot on the back of my head.

After that first week, I no longer felt so lucky to be alive. Instead I asked, *Why did I live?*

Through this ordeal, Matisse called me almost every day to see how I was doing. He returned to New York from overseas, but on his way to Philadelphia to see me he got into a fender-bender and ended up tending to that for the rest of the day.

In typical thoughtful Matisse style, he surprised me by having his driver and black Town Car arrive to bring me back to New York. He was always so thoughtful, kind, and generous. Seeing the driver standing so properly at the door did make me smile.

But I wasn't ready to leave Philadelphia. I had doctor's appointments, and I could not think of riding in a car for two hours—too much pain and PTSD.

I had to wait. I was on my own. Completely on my own.

After two months in Philadelphia, I couldn't take it anymore. I had to get back to New York. The train was definitely not an option. I have never set foot on a train since the accident. I doubt I ever will.

Instead, I called a cab, the only option I had. Yet, even that was grueling. I call it the Hell Ride, lying on the back seat in utter terror, sensing every movement and crying, fearing that any moment we would spin out of control. I would cringe at every bump. At every brake, I thought I would die. Road noises sounded like thunder.

When we got to the Lincoln Tunnel, I sat up with a start, reawakening my screaming shoulder pain. I smelled gas fumes. Suddenly my heart was racing and I couldn't breathe. This was Car Three all over again—no exits, no escape route.

"Can't you go faster?" I gasped, gripping the back of the driver's seat. "We have to get out! We have to get out of here!"

"Lady, can't you see the cars in front of me?" Frustration showed on every line of his olive face. He stared at me in the rearview mirror.

The old Lynn loved scuba diving, zip lining, and indoor skydiving. She'd even tried the trapeze. The new Lynn could no longer ride in a moving vehicle of any type without abject panic. Always on alert for exit signs and directions on how to get out, I saw no way of escape in the tunnel.

When we reached open sky again, I collapsed on the back seat, my insides quivering and my tears pooling on the brown upholstery under my cheek. "I can't live like this!" I screamed in my head.

At the penthouse, the bellman helped me with my few things. I broke into a cold sweat in the elevator. With the doors closed, there wasn't enough oxygen for eight people. The doors sealed shut. No way out.

Slowly the numbers changed. Why was the penthouse on the 25th floor? I looked up for air holes. Was there an escape hatch? How would we get out of here?

I wanted out. Really, another stop? More people? I started to hyperventilate and tried to hide it from the other people in the elevator.

Matisse hurried to greet me when I stepped off the elevator. It felt so good to be in his arms again. Maybe here I could rest and recover.

Immediately the question, "What happened that night? You've only given me snippets on the phone. Take me through it step by step."

All I could do was sob and shake my head. Matisse put his arm around me, and we moved into the bedroom where Marta helped me change and get into bed. She handed me two pain pills and a glass of water.

I slept for the first time in weeks.

When I woke up, I was totally alone in the dark penthouse. Marta had gone out and Matisse had a dinner party that evening. I shook with terror and sobbed hysterically. Finally,

I crawled under the bed, seeking safety in a primal way.

When Matisse came home, he began opening doors looking for me. I made a noise as

I inched across the carpet to come out.

"What are you doing?" he asked, helping me up. His expression was part concern and part dismay.

I sobbed, "I don't know. I don't know."

The next day he found me a psychiatrist, a physical therapist, and a host of other professionals to help me get back on my feet. Meanwhile I canceled tennis and dance classes, and took a giant step back from life as I knew it.

My "new normal" was a living nightmare.

Chapter 11

Recovery is Relative

Over the next months, I stayed in a constant state of mindless panic, afraid of being alone, afraid of any moving vehicle, afraid of the elevator but too sick to take the stairs. I had weekly medical and therapy appointments and had to take Valium® just to get down to the street. Taxi rides were pure torture.

The girls were also panicked. They would no longer ride the train, our point of connection between New York and Philadelphia. Without the train, the ninety-minute commute turned into hours on the bus or in a cab. I did my best to maintain our weekend visits but the entire process was an endurance test that left me shaking, sobbing, and exhausted.

Seeing me in that state upset Marilyn and Brigitte to the point that I wondered if my visits only made things worse for them.

Over time I learned more details about the accident. Seven cars and the engine made up Amtrak 188 with 238 passengers, 8 of them Amtrak employees[13]. Of that number, 8 passengers lost their lives,[14] 46 were critically injured,[15] and 113 more had other injuries[16]. Airborne luggage and seats slammed our bodies at more than 100 miles per hour[17]. On that stretch of track near Port Richmond, the speed limit was 50 mph[18] because of a sharp curve ahead, the sharpest curve on the Northeastern corridor.[19] The engineer had accelerated to 106 mph, more than twice the safe speed, and the train derailed at the curve.[20]

Reports said that at the last minute the engineer threw on the emergency brake.[21] What would happen to a car traveling at more than 100 mph if someone suddenly put on the emergency brake? It would

13 https://mobile.nytimes.com/2016/01/31/magazine/the-wreck-of-amtrak-188.html

14 https://mobile.nytimes.com/2015/05/15/us/eight-amtrak-passengers-deaths-echo-across-the-region-and-the-world.html

15 https://www.washingtonpost.com/local/trafficandcommuting/ntsb-expected-to-conclude-that-engineer-in-deadly-2015-amtrak-derailment-lost-track-of-where-he-was/2016/05/17/17c45356-1c35-11e6-9c81-4be1c14fb8c8_story.html

16 Ibid.

17 https://www.nytimes.com/interactive/2016/05/17/us/amtrak-train-crash-derailment-philadelphia.html

18 Ibid.

19 http://abc7ny.com/news/ntsb-amtrak-engineer-distracted-during-deadly-philly-crash/1341055/

20 https://www.nytimes.com/interactive/2016/05/17/us/amtrak-train-crash-derailment-philadelphia.html

21 http://abc7ny.com/news/ntsb-amtrak-engineer-distracted-during-deadly-philly-crash/1341055/

flip, again and again. No wonder Car One was crumpled into a lump of twisted metal and Cars 2 and 3 overturned.

It didn't make sense. Thinking about it made my brain hurt. I couldn't deal with it and shut it out.

My constant pain and the mental fog from pain meds meant I couldn't maintain my recruiting business. My client list shrank to a handful of people who had been with me for years. Each cab ride to Philadelphia cost me $200. My credit cards quickly maxed out as my expenses skyrocketed and my income went into a downward spiral. I was too proud to let anyone know the financial trouble I was in, even Matisse. If he had known, he would have been appalled.

Looking back, I can see how my frantic busy-ness was a way to hide my distress. If I stayed in constant motion, I wouldn't have to look at the mounting medical bills, or my bank statements, or anything that upset me. With the constant brain fog and the blur of pain medicine, it was easy to ignore. Yet, deep inside I felt a growing dread.

With so much anxiety, I found myself taking more and more prescription drugs just trying to cope. Before the accident I didn't even take aspirin. Now, between the pain meds, tranquilizers, anti-inflammatories and other prescriptions—I was taking pills by the handful while still in physical agony, riddled with fear, and overwhelmed by PTSD.

I couldn't bear to look at myself in the mirror. Dark sunken eyes stared back at me with nameless dread. Pain lines seamed my face. My beautiful long blond hair had permanently vanished from the back of my head.

Eventually, I had a hairpiece made. Matisse laughingly called it my "lady toupee."

I wasn't laughing.

I couldn't work, but since my business didn't carry disability insurance I had no money coming in. Matisse generously helped me, hoping the vivacious, happy, capable woman he loved would eventually reappear. Unfortunately, that woman never got off the train.

This new Lynn bore not the slightest resemblance to her. The strain soon affected our relationship. I could no longer fly six hours to Europe. He traveled alone while I grew more and more depressed. I got so sick of staying at home, but my fear kept me there. That made me angry. *I want my life back, damn it!*

One afternoon in September Leslie, Leila and I were on our way to see BFF #3 Linda Dunne perform with her band *The Four Bitchin' Babes*. Linda's another Academy of Notre Dame grad. Leslie put the trip together to cheer me up. Who can be depressed listening to songs like "Bridesmaid Dress" and "The Boob Fairy"?

Unfortunately, the trip to the event wasn't a happy one. I sort of (absolutely) had a meltdown on the way. Thankfully, Leslie was driving her SUV. I was riding shotgun, with Leila in the back.

"What am I going to do?" I sobbed. "My whole life is in a death spiral. I can't pull myself together. Why can't I PULL MYSELF TOGETHER?!"

Leila leaned forward to put her hand on my arm, "Lynn, this is where you bounce. You've gotta hit bottom… then below bottom where you care less, when you have nothing left and nothing left to lose. This is your time, my friend."

I stopped crying and looked at her as though seeing her for the first time. Leila had lost her two brothers. She had been through hell and back, and look at her—a successful financial planner with a wonderful marriage of more than twenty years, always positive and upbeat no matter what. She became my role model that day.

Looking back, I'm grateful. I grew so much because I know what it feels like to hit bottom.

In October, I made an announcement while we were enjoying Marta's excellent steamed lobster and lemon thyme butter. She had turned the lighting low, and we had a short candle between us on the creamy tablecloth.

"I'm going with you to your party in the Hamptons," I said, trying to sound casual though my heart was thumping. "Leila and Leslie are driving up. It will be fun."

Matisse paused in mid-bite. "Are you sure you're up to it?"

I nodded. "I've got to snap out of this sometime, Matisse. I feel like a zombie, and I hate that feeling."

He touched his napkin to his lips. "If you're sure you're up to it, I'm happy to see you make this step." He smiled into my eyes, "I've missed you." But still he seemed different, as if had plans that didn't include me. I told myself I was just imagining it.

Matisse was hosting a few friends, only a hundred-fifty or so, at his place in the Hamptons. This was our local crowd, and I just had to be there. This party signified the start of my comeback – I WOULD do this.

The day before the party, we drove to the twelve-bedroom house. I assisted Marta with preparations as much as I could—which I always did—and felt exhausted by time to dress. Marta helped me into a sparkly halter top and amazing white pants with heels to die for. The halter went on easily with no sleeves to work through.

We spent half an hour straightening my long hair and getting my hairpiece set right. My limited range of motion made it impossible for me to style my hair or zip my dress. I had to have help. Yet the result looked impressive. I was ready to conquer. The home was amazing that night, like Nikki Beach® in Marbella, Spain. The candles and lighting made a lasting impression on me.

Just before eight, Matisse arrived in my dressing room looking debonair in his Brioni® tux and black bow tie. As he opened the door, I unstrapped my sling with a loud Velcro noise.

"What are you doing?" Matisse asked, worried.

"I don't want to wear the sling. Everyone will ask me about my injury… and the train crash."

He shook his head. "You need to wear it, Lynn. You'll end up hurting yourself worse."

Nothing could convince me. I went down without it. I looked at all the amazing outfits and all the friends he had been traveling with for the past six months (sadly without me). It was a tough year for poor Matisse, but he was never alone or lonely. He had so many great friends who kept me informed of his adventures. Somewhere along the way the stories got confusing or facts went missing, but I loved to listen and imagine being there.

The crowd looked like something right out of *The Great Gatsby*, or a movie set. The women with glittering jewels draped around their long thin necks, and the men swaggering in their perfectly-fitted tuxes. They were the very definition of glamor.

It felt so good to mingle with people and catch up on the latest news. At last I felt almost normal. I met some new people, including Chandler Huffington, a real estate Moghul, art expert, and philanthropist. He was tall, dark and amazingly built. And those blue eyes that spoke to your soul without saying a thing. He held a highball glass filled with Don Julio 1942.™

Chandler's eyes zoomed in on me when he walked by. I instantly zinged with some type of connection or chemistry. But then again, I am sure every other lady in the room did as well. He knew how to speak and send out caring vibes so she'd feel like the only person in the room.

When Matisse introduced me I felt my face grow warm, Chandler looked me over admiringly and said to Matisse, "Why is she with you?" He kissed my hand in a lingering way and said, "I'd love to host you at my home in the Bahamas anytime you are down there."

I looked at Matisse.

Matisse said, "Oh, we would love to."

Chandler looked at me and said, "If she wants to bring you along."

Confused, I laughed and looked at Matisse.

Wow. On the one hand I was beyond flattered. On the other hand, I wasn't so sure what had just happened.

Chandler had a crowd with him all evening. The men wanted to be him, and the women… well, yes he had a few choices that evening and any evening, I am sure.

I stayed at the party as long as I could. Matisse introduced me as Lynn. Just Lynn, not girlfriend or partner. That upset me.

Around ten o'clock the pain in my shoulder grew so severe that I broke down in tears, and I went to my room.

The rest of the evening I spent lying in our quiet bedroom away from everyone, praying the pain meds would kick in, crying from discomfort and disappointment.

When Matisse came in around 2 a.m., he shook his head at the sight of me sprawled on the bed, still in my party clothes, with my head on the sheet. I could no longer sleep with a pillow.

"I tried to tell you, Lynn. If you had worn the sling you wouldn't be in so much pain."

I rolled over so he could help me undress. Easing out of the outfit, I got into my favorite pink silk nightie without his help. I kept my face turned away until he shut off the light.

Over the next nine months, I tried to get back on track, working harder and harder at trying to please him by decorating his new house while he was overseas. I spent hours meeting with designers, looking over curtains, dishes, glassware, rugs, art, and outside furniture. I spent hours making decisions, unpacking boxes, fixing things, and making the place beautiful. We had different tastes, Matisse and I, but I tried to find lovely things we both enjoyed.

He was thrilled with the end result. It felt nice to put time into a home we'd enjoy for years to come. I was doing this for us, for our future. All the time decorating, shopping, and planning, took away precious hours from my business. I knew it was temporary, though. If I could just get through this year with the new home and planning a few big parties, I could go back to working next year. I could still do it all.

But I couldn't do it all. The old Lynn was gone. Instead, I ended up in a downward spiral of pain and exhaustion that created a vortex of angry outbursts and blaming whenever Matisse was around. Not a good scene for either of us.

Matisse's trips to New York became fewer and farther between. Sometimes four months would go by before he returned. He still loved to travel so he did, and took other friends along with him. I don't think he stayed long enough to see the changes in me or to realize how deep they ran. I would never be the same.

When he was in town, we'd often end up fighting. I tried to work and keep up with his needs, the parties, dinners, theater, and events while running my six businesses.

But I was spinning in place. Nothing was truly accomplished. Every task was left in some level of incompleteness. I was stressed. I was alone. I was falling deeper and deeper into debt trying to invest in myself and my businesses while spending thousands on medical bills. The harder I tried, the more I failed.

Finally, the hammer fell in August, 2016. Matisse and I were in Las Vegas to attend a wedding and for my birthday celebration. I'd known for months that things were going downhill, but I maintained hope that we'd pull through it. It was not an easy year for either of us. He was not there to help me, or see my struggles, or how hard I was working. I was not the delightful travelling companion he craved. I loved Matisse completely and absolutely. I couldn't imagine life without him, so I didn't let myself go there.

He gave me an orange Hermes® Birkin bag for my birthday. It matched the scarf from the year before. He held my hand after he gave it to me. He was always so thoughtful.

I expected him to say something sweet, like he always did, but instead he said, "This is the end." He had tears in his eyes.

My heart lurched. "What?" I gasped.

His expression hardened. "We need to go our own separate ways. I need a break from this."

"But where will I go? I sold my home."

He shrugged. "You'll be okay, Lynn. You are always good at figuring things out."

And that was that. My troubles and I were no longer of concern to him.

We still had two days before the flight home. I went through the motions, attending events and trying to act normal, but I was reeling. The old Lynn would have come up with a plan and steps to follow. The old Lynn would have fixed this. The new Lynn didn't have a clue.

We flew back to New York together. Matisse would leave for Europe the next day.

I slept in the guest room that night. The next day I came to the living room as he was waiting for the elevator, hoping against hope that he had changed his mind.

He smiled when he saw me. For a moment he was the sweet man I had fallen in love with three years before. The man I was still in love with.

When I reached him, he said, "I am sorry this didn't work out, Lynn. Nothing is forever. I can help you for a bit to get you going.

Get in touch with Caren while I am away and put a plan together for where you want to go from here."

He knew I had moved in to be with him forever. He knew I had moved away from my girls because of the promise of a better life for us all. He knew this was the worst possible timing for an ending. His glistening eyes told me I would be ok.

I felt a glimmer of hope when he scooped me close for a long deep kiss. Hugging me, he said, "Maybe I'll drive down to see you sometime." Then he stepped into the elevator and the doors slid closed.

At that moment, I knew in my heart that he would never look back.

I *do* look back, though, and I know that the end of our relationship had happened a long time before. I was fundamentally changed from the woman who had shared his home, who had built a life with him.

He tried. I tried. All the effort in the world was not enough to fix the damage that had been done. Too many cracks in the foundation until the structure finally crumbled. Not every victim of Amtrak 188 was flesh and blood. Our relationship is proof of that. I'm sure we weren't the only ones to break up.

I don't know how I managed to breathe over the next two days. Packing with my shoulder screaming, my anxiety through the roof, labeling boxes for shipping… *to where?*

My mother lived in Philadelphia. She had a spare bedroom.

One phone call and I was moving back in with my Mom. At my age.

The taxi ride to Philadelphia seemed endless. Tears oozed down my cheeks in a wide stream. Zac Brown's "Highway 20 Ride" came over the radio and that was too much. *"You may hate me. Mom and I could never get along."*

I bawled uncontrollably. I thought I was Cinderella, but no fairy godmother had appeared to keep me from face-planting on the pavement. Why did I move to New York? Why did I fool myself with fairy tales? What kind of mom does that? The divorce was tough on the kids, and now this! Marilyn and Brigitte loved Matisse, too. They would be devastated.

My breakup with Matisse was so much worse than my divorce because I was already in such a bad place in my life. After my divorce, I still had a home and a great career. I was healthy and active. I knew where I was going. Here I couldn't begin to imagine my next steps. Just waking up brought a crushing weight to my chest.

I questioned my decisions. Moving to New York had seemed such a good idea at the time, but that one decision changed the course of my life. All the fun, the travel, the beautiful people—all the advantages for the girls and the business connections for me—how quickly they had disappeared after I was hurt and could no longer maintain the "lifestyle." The party bus kept on moving. Anyone who couldn't keep up got left behind.

It's a shame that I didn't understand that before. Things would have gone so much differently if I had stayed in my house with my girls in Philadelphia. They say love is blind, but what a cruel thing to have the blinders yanked off so ruthlessly.

Chapter 12

Train Safety

After all the stress and trauma from the train crash, my breakup with Matisse was the most devastating of all. I truly had given him my whole heart, for what I thought was forever. My sweet future vanished, and I had no idea where to go from here. How could I pick up the pieces and move on when my life was completely shattered—physically, mentally, emotionally. My career and family structure were damaged almost beyond repair.

I was at the bottom. No, below bottom.

Leila and Leslie—and my kids—were my lifeline. They'd stop by to pull me out of the house at least once a week. What would I have done without them? Often, we'd sit in a coffee shop and chatter. Sometimes we walked the mall or went to a movie. When I was spinning out with pain and discouragement, they would get me back in focus and make me laugh all at the same time.

A select few of my global friends did stay in touch. They are cherished gems who saw my heart chose to stick with me during my stopover at the bottom—family contacts, business contacts, and personal friends who gave emotional support to me and my girls on a daily basis. That's what life is about, isn't it? Connecting and paying it forward? I am still a kindhearted giver like my dad, maybe a bit more cautious, but I still try to help people. I guess it's my flaw. Not such a bad flaw, I think.

When I reached Philadelphia, I got off the pain meds to help clear my head. I threw myself into rebuilding my business and writing. I reconnected with my amazing local friends. They all asked how they could help. This was the supportive culture I was used to, where I could thrive.

I got up the nerve to call Chandler Huffington, the real estate Moghul with the soulful eyes. When he heard the story of my breakup he said, "I never said he was smart."

That made me laugh for first time in what seemed forever.

"When are you coming to the Bahamas?" he asked. "Life will be okay."

Maybe, just maybe, he was right. Perhaps life could be okay again.

This entire journey has been such a learning experience in so many ways. My main lesson? It's always better to live in reality than have a dream world pop like a soap bubble, leaving nothing behind but air. I resolved to keep my feet firmly planted on the ground and my eyes wide open in my emerging future.

During this time, I started researching the train crash. Car One had torn away from the engine and folded into an L shape[22], splitting open and spitting passengers out into the night.[23] One man woke up under an upturned wheel.[24] A girl landed near a tree.[25] Four people in that car lost their lives.

A light pole impaled Car Two and brought it to a sudden halt.[26] One passenger instantly became a quadriplegic.[27]

Car Three overturned and four more people died. Car Four had tilted, resulting in flying debris wounding those inside. The remaining three cars had remained upright, those inside badly jolted, but comparatively untouched.

Eight dead, forty-six critically injured, and hundreds with broken bones, wrenched bodies, and shattered minds. None of us would ever see the world the same again. None of us were the same after the night of May 12, 2015.

Chaos and confusion had left hapless unsuspecting people trapped in the dark in pain and shock with no idea how to exit the car. The end doors were locked. Smoke filled the cars. Fluorescent tape on the floor became when the floor became a side wall. Luggage and broken seats filled the aisles, making the inside of that space impossible to navigate.

22 http://www.philly.com/philly/news/special_packages/Amtrak_Car_1_
    survivors_speak_about_their_recovery_a_year_later.html
23 https://www.nytimes.com/interactive/2016/05/17/us/amtrak-train-crash-
    derailment-philadelphia.html?_r=1
24 http://www.philly.com/philly/news/special_packages/Amtrak_Car_1_
    survivors_speak_about_their_recovery_a_year_later.html
25 Ibid.
26 http://www.fireengineering.com/articles/print/volume-168/issue-10/
    features/amtrak-derailment-operations-the-first-24-minutes.html
27 http://people.com/human-interest/chef-eli-kulp-paralyzed-in-deadly-
    amtrak-derailment/

Most of all, the passengers were unprepared. Even passengers trained in emergency response were unprepared in how to survive a train crash.

Why? The airlines have safety training before every flight with marked exits and emergency lighting in case of a power failure. We had nothing like that on the train, no announcements, no safety procedures were recited to us. We were in pitch darkness with no idea how to get out, milling around trying to save our own lives without a clear course of action laid out for us.

I started asking people, "How would you get out of a train in an emergency?" I was checking for public awareness. "It's not a joke. Do you know? Let's imagine it's dark outside and your train flipped over. It's filling with smoke. Tell me what you would do. Where are the windows? How do they open? Do you know?"

One hundred percent of the time, their answer: "I don't have a clue."

Late in 2016, I had my "Erin Brockovich moment" while I was watching a video on Today.com about railroad safety called "How to Get Out of a Train Accident Alive."[28] It was originally posted the day after Amtrak 188 crashed.

In the year before the crash, there were 2,100 collisions and 230 people killed on the rails. That started as a burning in my soul and ended up with a strong determination to kick some ass. I am very competitive. I rowed while at Villanova and won the Dad Vail Regatta medal twice while Leila cheered me on to the finish line.

---

28 https://www.today.com/video/how-to-get-out-of-a-train-accident-alive-444578371741

I made a list of things that didn't work in our attempt to get out of the train and asked Leila and Leslie for input the next time we got together for Happy Hour. They keep me grounded.

"I've been working on my safety awareness campaign," I said, sipping my iced tea. "So,

I wrote a list of changes for the railway companies based on what happened in the train crash."

I dug in my purse. "Here it is. This is the 'What Didn't Work' list." I put it on the table between us. We were in a black booth near the back of the tavern. This early in the evening, we had the place to ourselves.

Leslie picked up the page, and Leila leaned closer to look at it with her.

Leslie nodded, "This is pretty basic. I like that. 'People can't read complicated signs in the dark.'"

"Or in a smoky car," Leila added.

"'Orange glow tape on the floor is useless when the floor is upside down.'" Leslie read. "Tell me about it."

"It seems so simple to us," I said. "But most people don't think in those terms."

Leila picked up her drink. "I wonder how many people making up the safety features have actually been in a train wreck."

"We had to jump ten feet down, and we were already hurt," I said. "If there were safety features to help us, we knew nothing of them. I think something like a safety ladder on the roof would have helped prevent a lot more damage to people."

Leslie nodded. "They need to think of how the train would be on its side, upside down, dark, smoky, whatever and put glowing arrows or something everywhere."

"We were shocked and disoriented. We needed a beacon to show us the way out."

After talking with Leslie and Leila about how much this information is needed, I became obsessed with train safety.

I began a mission to find the truth about the crash of Amtrak 188 and devoted every waking moment to research. I read every article, listened to hundreds of news recordings, and watched YouTube until I couldn't see straight. My brother Robert was my chief supporter and head research assistant. He'd stop by after work, and we'd talk about the crash, sharing information and running scenarios. Robert's reporting expertise helped me to narrow and refine my research. We discovered a story about an oil train disaster in Montreal. Oil trains derailed and the explosions destroyed half of an entire town.[29]

I read each passenger and first responder story. I wanted to know more about the lives of everyone involved. They were my new family through experience. On the one-year anniversary, I came across a story about a chef in Car Two, who was rendered a quadriplegic from his injuries.[30] His story was one of many tragedies that night.

Reports maintained mechanical failure was not the issue since the engine, ACS-64 Cities Sprinter 601, was only one year old.[31] The locomotive data recorder showed that the train accelerated as it approached the Frankford Junction curve when it should have slowed to 50 mph.[32] Bostian claimed he couldn't remember anything for several moments before the train reached the curve.[33]

29 https://en.wikipedia.org/wiki/Lac-M%C3%A9gantic_rail_disaster
30 http://people.com/human-interest/chef-eli-kulp-paralyzed-in-deadly-amtrak-derailment/

The data recorder also showed that he had hit the emergency brake while going 106 miles per hour.[34] That accounted for the shaking of the car and the pandemonium that happened immediately afterward. Later I learned this is a standard emergency procedure called "dumping the brakes."[35] It's the last resort for slowing a runaway train. Unfortunately for the passengers of 188, it was too little, too late.

Investigators questioned Bostian about his training, his personal routines, his sleep habits and even how he got to work. He had no drugs or alcohol in his system, and he had not been on his cell phone.[36]

Thinking back to my own memory of that evening, the train had been a few minutes late leaving the station. That's why I was on board. If Amtrak 188 had been on time, I would have missed the train.

On a quiet Saturday two weeks after Christmas, Robert, Leila and I were sitting at Mom's dining room table drinking coffee and eating chocolate cupcakes. We were scrolling through pictures of the crash, discussing my idea of writing a book about railroad safety.

Suddenly, Robert called out, "Wait a minute! Go back to the last picture."

31 https://en.wikipedia.org/wiki/2015_Philadelphia_train_derailment
32 https://en.wikipedia.org/wiki/2015_Philadelphia_train_
    derailment#Investigation
33 http://www.cnn.com/2015/05/14/us/amtrak-engineer-who-is-brandon-
    bostian/index.html
34 https://en.wikipedia.org/wiki/2015_Philadelphia_train_
    derailment#Investigation
35 https://en.wikipedia.org/wiki/Emergency_brake_(train)
36 http://heavy.com/news/2015/05/brandon-bostian-amtrak-philadelphia-
    crash-derail-derailment-engineer-name-gay-police-statement-photos-
    video-speed-speeding-victims-conductor/

I clicked and leaned in for a closer look. "What?"

"Do you see that?" he asked. "Oil tankers right there next to Car Two."[37]

"Yeah," I said, remembering. "I saw them that night.[38] We were smelling oil from the moment of the crash. And we walked right by a long line of tankers on our way out."

"Look at YouTube, the videos of the crash. See the tankers right there near the train?"[39]

I looked at an image in the right column with the headline "Lac-Mégantic Rail Disaster" dated July 7, 2013.[40] I clicked. "OMG, Look! They had the exact curve matching the one in Port Richmond. If you put our train curves side by side, they match. Half the town burned up. That could have been Philadelphia!" I stared, trying to wrap my head around it.

Robert leaned in to read the article. In a moment, he looked up. "Do you know what would have happened if you had hit those tankers?" Robert asked. "The Montreal disaster was only one train, and it took out half the town. There were five trains next to Amtrak 188.[41]" He shivered and took a breath. "I feel like someone just walked over my grave."

---

37 http://www.philly.com/philly/news/special_packages/Amtrak_Car_1_
    survivors_speak_about_their_recovery_a_year_later.html
38 http://www.fireengineering.com/articles/print/volume-168/issue-10/
    features/amtrak-derailment-operations-the-first-24-minutes.html
39 https://www.youtube.com/results?search_query=amtrak+188+crash
40 https://en.wikipedia.org/wiki/Lac-M%C3%A9gantic_rail_disaster
41 http://www.phillymag.com/citified/2015/05/13/amtrak-crash-oil-tankers/

Chapter 13

Bomb Trains

The following Friday evening, Robert strode into Mom's house holding a file folder and his tablet under his arm. "Hey! How's it going?" he asked, his typical greeting. He wore a navy overcoat and leather gloves this chilly evening.

"Hi Robert!" Mom called from the couch. "I saw you on TV tonight. Handsome as ever."

I looked up from my laptop, pleased to see him. "What did you bring me?" I asked, eyeing the folder.

"Just wait and see!" he said. Pulling off his gloves, he circled the room to kiss Mom before joining me at the table. The Windsor chair next to me made a scraping sound as he pulled it back.

He set the folder and tablet on the table. "Take a look at these. I printed some articles about "bomb trains." That is, trains hauling tanker cars carrying particularly explosive forms of crude oil, such as Bakken crude."[42] He pulled a page from the stack. "Aerial photos. Not one… Not two… Count them. Five oil trains lined up beside your crash site.[43] If your train had kept going one second more, and hit those tankers…"

I took the paper from him. The room started spinning.

His voice pulled me back. I tried to focus. *What was he saying?*

"Lynn. Lynn! Tell me what you remember after you got off the train. Close your eyes and remember."

I winced. "I don't like to remember it. I've been blocking it out for a year and a half."

"Close your eyes, Lynn."

Grimacing, I took two deep breaths and tried to relax. "I smelled oil. And soot," I opened my eyes to look at him. "They treated me for soot inhalation at the hospital."

"And…" He waved his hand like a hypnotist I once saw in Vegas. *Deeper and deeper.*

42 https://www.google.com/search?rlz=1C1CHWA_enUS633US635&q=bomb+train+definition&oq=bomb+train+definition&gs_l=psy-ab.3...279496.282870.0.283662.21.20.0.0.0.0.212.2029.0j15j1.16.0....0...1.1.64.psy-ab..5.15.1816...0j35i39k1j0i67k1j0i10k1j0i22i30k1j33i21k1._jHrqIYwWMo

43 http://www.phillymag.com/citified/2015/05/13/amtrak-crash-oil-tankers/

Leaning back in my seat, getting into it now, I said, "Smoke. Someone screamed the train was on fire. We were choking on smoke and had to get out fast."

He murmured, "In the yard. What did you see?"

"A long row of black tankers all the way down."[44]

"Any flames?"

I shook my head. "Only smoke."

"Okay. Let's just say the engine did hit an oil tanker. What would happen?" He waited for my answer.

"An explosion."

"And a chain reaction," he added. "When one car explodes, others will follow." He let out a puff of air. "Thank God that didn't happen."

"But what if it was an empty tanker that got hit?" I asked. "Would it blow?"

"Maybe. But maybe it would just smolder and be done." He pulled another article from the file and pointed to yellow highlighting. "People from the neighborhood saw a flash of light."[45] He handed the paper to me.

I glanced at it and put it on the table. "Someone shouted the train was on fire," I said, nodding. I flicked through the saved photos on my laptop. "But no pictures of smoldering wreckage. Odd."

I stopped. "Wait! Look at the engine. It has a red streak down the side. We sideswiped something red. No one has mentioned that." I

44 http://www.phillymag.com/citified/2015/05/13/amtrak-crash-oil-tankers/
45 http://www.latimes.com/nation/la-na-amtrak-witnesses-20150513-story.
    html

peered at the screen. "Look at the soot along the top. See that? The roof looks burned… and black oil smeared on the outside of the engine."[46]

Robert added, "The engine landed so far ahead of the rest of the cars. Wouldn't the cars slam into the engine when the brakes went on? I don't see damage from photos." He paused, thinking. "When brakes locked down, did that automatically release the cars from the engine?"

"The front bottom of the engine has a huge chunk missing.[47] No one mentions what that impact was."

He nodded. "You've got me intrigued. My reporter nose might be smelling a cover up."

"Five oil trains lined up on the tracks and a runaway passenger train. Doesn't that sound newsworthy to you?" I asked.

"But by dawn the next morning, the scene was completely changed," he added. "The oil tankers are far back and no one's talking about them."[48] He shuffled through his manila folder. "I printed this as well," he said, handing over another page. "See?"

I scanned the paper. On February 1, 2015, less than six weeks before Amtrak 188 crashed, eleven oil tanker cars derailed in South Philadelphia.[49] Almost exactly a year earlier seven oil tankers derailed

46 http://a.abcnews.com/images/Nightline/150514_ntl_
   amtrak_1239_16x9_992.jpg
47 https://www.washingtonpost.com/graphics/local/amtrak-derail/img/aerial-
   4-photo-a.jpg?c=1df1da6
48 http://nicholasstixuncensored.blogspot.com/2015/05/amtrak-engineer-
   was-driving-train-188.html
49 http://6abc.com/news/11-train-cars-derail-in-south-philadelphia/498800/

over the Schuylkill River. The tanker cars were hanging off a bridge right above the river.[50]

As we dug deeper, we came across a site at PhillyMag.com with several articles on bomb trains and Bakken crude.[51] That's when things went from scary to horrifying.

Located in North Dakota, the Bakken Formation[52] produces crude oil that's different from typical crude.[53] They ship the crude in massive trains that string together more than 100 tanker cars[54], each one holding 30,000 gallons of oil.[55] That's more than 3 Million gallons of oil traveling through densely populated areas and near water resources.[56] These tanker trains often run parallel to passenger trains, sometimes sharing the same tracks.[57]

Because of the Bakken oil boom, 450,000 tanker trains of crude crossed the U.S. and Canada in 2015. In 2009 that number was just 9,500.[58] Rail lines that have been out of service for years are back in use, as well as old tanker cars taken out of retirement. Regulators have cited tanker cars made before 2011 as dangerously prone to puncture.[59] Old equipment means breakdowns, malfunctions and accidents. How is monitoring this? Who is in charge?

50 http://www.phillymag.com/news/2015/02/02/philadelphia-crude-oil-bomb-trains/
51 http://www.phillymag.com/search-results/?q=bomb+trains
52 https://en.wikipedia.org/wiki/Bakken_Formation
53 https://www.wsj.com/articles/no-headline-available-1393197890
54 http://www.latimes.com/nation/la-na-oil-train-explosions-20150313-story.html
55 https://en.wikipedia.org/wiki/Lac-M%C3%A9gantic_rail_disaster
56 https://news.vice.com/video/bomb-trains-the-crude-gamble-of-oil-by-rail
57 http://www.phillymag.com/citified/2015/05/13/amtrak-crash-oil-tankers

I went back to the Lac-Mégantic disaster. According to Wikipedia[60], on July 6, 2013, Lac-Mégantic in Quebec saw the effects of a bomb train when explosions from a derailed tanker train killed 47 people and destroyed half the town. A video on YouTube showed the blaze.[61]

In Lac-Mégantic, the derailment caused a series of massive explosions, including Boiling Liquid Expanding Vapor Explosions (BLEVE).[62] As liquid crude boils, the tank builds up pressure until it explodes, throwing shrapnel and burning oil hundreds of yards in all directions.[63]

After the fireballs, hundreds of thousands of gallons of boiling Bakken oil spilled through the streets and into the sewers of Lac-Mégantic. Explosions in the sewers blew manhole covers over thirty feet into the air and spewed burning oil that melted streetlamps.[64] Thousands of gallons of oil flowed into rivers and lakes and soaked deep into the ground.

For days, toxic fumes kept first responders from getting close to the crash site. Many of the missing were vaporized. Emergency Rooms remained eerily empty, a spooky silence that went to the bone. There were no wounded. Only corpses.[65]

58 https://www.nbcnews.com/news/us-news/heimdal-north-dakota-evacuated-after-fiery-oil-train-crash-n354686
59 https://news.vice.com/video/bomb-trains-the-crude-gamble-of-oil-by-rail
60 https://en.wikipedia.org/wiki/Lac-M%C3%A9gantic_rail_disaster
61 https://youtu.be/wVMNspPc8Zc
62 https://en.wikipedia.org/wiki/Boiling_liquid_expanding_vapor_explosion
63 Ibid.
64 https://en.wikipedia.org/wiki/Lac-M%C3%A9gantic_rail_disaster
65 https://www.thestar.com/news/canada/2013/07/07/lac_megantic_hospital_eerily_quiet_after_quebec_explosion.html

"Oh my God!" I cried. "That could have been me."

"It could have been all of us," Robert said. "Can you imagine the devastation?"

"I'm writing a book on train safety, but this is turning into something more," I said. "It's giving me the creeps, Robert. I'm not sure I can go here." Scrolling through the results of my search, I said, "Do people know these explosions are happening in North America? Are we that greedy for profit we've thrown safety to the wind?" I continued scrolling, reading aloud.

"February 15, 2015, Gogama, Ontario."[66]

CLICK.

"Two days later, Mt. Carbon, West Virginia."[67]

CLICK.

"March 4, an explosion in Galena, Illinois, involving the newer safer tankers."[68]

CLICK.

"On May 6, just six days before Amtrak 188, an explosion in Heimdal, North Dakota."[69]

66 http://www.timminspress.com/2015/02/24/big-clean-up-lies-ahead-after-train-derailment

67 http://www.politico.com/story/2015/02/new-oil-train-explosion-stokes-new-call-for-safety-rules-115271

68 http://www.chicagotribune.com/chi-galena-train-derailment-20150305-story.html

69 https://www.nbcnews.com/news/us-news/heimdal-north-dakota-evacuated-after-fiery-oil-train-crash-n354686

I scrolled faster. "Can you believe this? Casselton, North Dakota[70]; Lynchburg, Virginia[71]; Aliceville, Alabama[72]… All involving major explosions and oil spills."

He said, "Pennsylvania had three accidents in densely populated areas—one near Pittsburgh[73] and two in Philadelphia, but none of them exploded.[74] Thank God." Robert leaned back. He looked pale. "Seventeen bomb train derailments in the last year."[75]

I reached for my coffee mug, "There's another way to think about this, you know."

I sipped. "I just happen to land in a train next to five tankers? It all could be a huge coincidence, or it may be time to wake up."

Every week 45 to 80 oil trains[76] averaging 100 tanker cars each[77], roll through Philadelphia neighborhoods. The South Philadelphia refinery is the nation's biggest single consumer of Bakken crude.[78]

Over 3.9 million Pennsylvania residents live inside the half-mile evacuation corridor.[79] Philadelphia has 710,000 people within the zone from the suburbs to University City, Southwest Philadelphia, North Philadelphia and Center City.[80] Evacuating these areas would be a nightmare, resulting in massive casualties.

---

70 https://news.vice.com/video/bomb-trains-the-crude-gamble-of-oil-by-rail
71 Ibid.
72 http://www.wbrc.com/story/23913896/train-derailment-causes-fire-and-crude-oil-spill-near-aliceville
3 https://stateimpact.npr.org/pennsylvania/2014/02/13/train-carrying-crude-oil-derails-in-western-pa/
74 Ibid.
75 http://www.chicagomag.com/Chicago-Magazine/May-2016/Bomb-Trains/

Robert threw his pages to the table. "Look at this! It's business as usual... Never mind. Nothing to worry about."

Loopholes in existing laws allow oil companies to stay under-insured for a worst-case scenario. For example, Quebec submitted a $400 Million claim following the Lac-Mégantic disaster, but the train company carried only $25 Million in insurance. A judge ruled the insurance payout should go to the victims' families.[81] Who rebuilt the town? Taxpayers.

Everyone else has to be fully covered in order stay in business. Why is this industry exempt?

Since 9/11, the FBI has issued many warnings about terrorism related to trains and derailments. Yet, nothing changes. Derailers are a device used to take a runaway train off the tracks to prevent a collision. Many of these derailers have been stolen from rail facilities around the country, according to FBI warnings as far back as 2003.[82]

76 http://www.thedailybeast.com/derailed-amtrak-cars-nearly-hit-bomb-train
77 http://www.latimes.com/nation/la-na-oil-train-explosions-20150313-story.html
78 Ibid.
79 http://pennenvironment.org/news/pae/new-report-oil-trains-put-over-39-million-pennsylvania-residents-living-evacuation-zone
80 Ibid.
81 https://www.thestar.com/news/canada/2014/06/16/quebec_claims_400_million_for_lacmgantic_train_disaster.html
82 http://www.thegatewaypundit.com/2015/05/flashback-fbi-warns-of-train-derailment-threat/

I read from the screen, "Someone who lives near the crash site said this, 'An Amtrak guy told me those tankers are full. If that engine hit that tanker[83], it would've set off an explosion like no other.'"[84]

"Look at these Twitter photos,"[85] Robert said, "I'd say that's less than fifty feet between Car Two and the nearest tanker."

"Why doesn't someone do something?" I asked. "There are plenty of photos showing my reality, how close we really were to disaster."

Robert shrugged. "All these accidents continue largely unaddressed[86], and local government has its hands tied."

We looked at a surveillance video of the crash.[87] I leaned closer to the screen, intrigued by something.

"Play that again. What was that brilliant flash? An explosion?"

His lips twitched and his eyes narrowed as he looked at the screen. "Could be a flash burn from a mostly empty car, or an electricity arc from the broken lines."

I took a breath. "We may never know what actually happened. But one thing I am certain of. No one is telling the whole truth. Philadelphia almost blew sky high that night and not a single person is talking about it."

---

83 http://www.cnn.com/2015/05/13/us/amtrak-train-derailment-passenger-accounts/index.html

84 Ibid.

85 https://twitter.com/RexBainbridge/status/598606625881137153/photo/1?ref_src=twsrc%5Etfw&ref_url=http%3A%2F%2Fwww.phillymag.com%2Fcitified%2F2015%2F05%2F13%2Famtrak-crash-oil-tankers%2F

86 https://news.vice.com/video/bomb-trains-the-crude-gamble-of-oil-by-rail

87 https://youtu.be/yV4julsxpVo

Suddenly, I gasped. "Look at that pole going through Car Two![88] That pole stopped the train. Otherwise we would have hit those tankers." My throat tightened, "I'm going to be sick." The fear and the flashbacks rolled over me.

As the panic attack subsided, it was replaced by that familiar burning in my chest—part anger and part ass-kicking vibes. I pulled my laptop closer to me. "Here is the real story that

I think should have been posted May 12, 2015." I clicked an app on my laptop. "I'm going to record what I say, so I can write it later."

Speaking into the laptop mike, I said:

"This is my city, my hometown. This is where I grew up. I'm a graduate of Villanova and the Academy of Notre Dame. My kids went to suburban Philadelphia schools. No one is more Philadelphia than I am.

"My kids could have been on that train with me. You and your family could have been on that train. But worse… If you were near Philadelphia on May 12, 2015, you might not be around to read this book.

"What would have happened if one steel bar did not get in the way? You see, the bar that sliced into Car Two saved the city when it stopped the train." I shifted in my chair and leaned closer to the laptop mike.

"What do you get when you take one train going 106 mph, add 1 sharp turn on the tracks and 5 tanker trains filled with oil?

"BOOM! Mass casualties everywhere. Every hospital is flooded. The city's closed down. Philadelphia becomes an instant war zone.

88 http://www.fireengineering.com/articles/print/volume-168/issue-10/ features/amtrak-derailment-operations-the-first-24-minutes.html

"Social media and bloggers have talked about bomb trains for years. They've produced documentaries and news articles. They have discussed this on online bulletin boards and chat rooms. Do a Google search, and you'll find them.[89]

"This might be a sad coincidence, but I am pointing out the elephant in the room. The press coverage on May 12, 2015, disappeared within hours. Later photos showed the oil tankers far away[90], and I bought into the false memory that the tankers were too distant to be dangerous. The truth? We came within feet of hitting five rows of tankers in a highly populated area.[91] Still, the world goes blissfully on.

"Knowing I was within seconds of death, I'm here to make sure the world sees these other photos, so people can draw their own conclusions. They might scare you. They might inspire you to act as well.

"If the headlines had reported 238 people killed from the train crash, hospitals flooded with 15,000 dead and wounded from the neighborhood, and 100,000 evacuated—would anyone listen then? If Philadelphia were on fire, the biggest oil ecological event ever—would anyone listen? What the heck are we doing? Does it take more body bags to bring about change?

"Who is orchestrating this madness?

"Could Amtrak 188 be a dress rehearsal for something more sinister?"

89 https://www.google.com/search?q=bomb+trains&rlz=1C1CHWA_
    enUS633US635&oq=bomb+trains&aqs=chrome..
    69i57j69i60l3j35i39j0.4159j0j4&sourceid=chrome&ie=UTF-8
90 http://www.businessinsider.com/here-everything-we-know-about-
    amtrak-188-train-wreck-in-philadelphia-2015-5
91 http://www.phillymag.com/citified/2015/05/13/amtrak-crash-oil-tankers/

Chapter 14

Forever Changed

Today, when people ask me about the train crash I tell them it was my personal wake-up call. It was a wake-up call to stay more present with my family, friends, and loved ones. I used to stay on my phone and devices, ignoring the really important people right in front of me. Now, I value my time with those I love. Every second is precious.

Before, I was sleepwalking. Now I walk and I see. I love sitting quietly to feel the sun. To stop and breathe. To notice.

I'm grateful, and I forgive.

My physical limitations are permanent. I don't sleep well. I have persistent brain fog. I can't zip my dress or sleep on a pillow, and I can no longer lift things. I live in constant pain from the permanent damage to my back and neck. I live in constant anxiety and quickly slip into fear.

My new life is very different. I used to stay in multi-tasking mode, but now I'm forced to slow down and focus on one task at a time. I am not who I used to be mentally or physically. I won't be.

Now, I am simply grateful I'm alive and focus on moving forward. I've learned where my true priorities lie. No more chasing imaginary rainbows toward an imaginary future. My feet are planted on terra firma for good. When I hit bottom, I followed Leila's advice and I bounced. I'm rebuilding my recruiting business, and I'm finishing a great script for my global awareness movie on dyslexia. My friends are solid and true. I know I can depend on them.

My girls have learned so much from my experiences. They both saw a change in me because of Matisse. That relationship was so different from my rocky marriage. They saw a man who spoke kindly, flattered me and brought flowers, who took me on trips and remembered birthdays, who never fought and always said I'm sorry and I love you. Both girls have found young men who speak nicely and treat them with respect, even in the midst of a disagreement. If my girls learned they deserve to be loved and cherished, then it has been worth it.

My ex-husband, Jeff, continues to support my kids and is a great dad.

Happy endings are possible, but they might look different than you expect. This Cinderella had to learn to save herself.

Life is a mixed bag. Every problem comes with a blessing. Every blessing comes with a problem. The old Lynn stayed on the fast track that kept getting faster and faster, with less and less happiness. Fate took me off the fast track and showed me what's truly important: People. Family and friends. Not just my own but the family and friends of every single American who steps foot on a train.

I will be the mouthpiece for those who died. I will not be silenced.

We matter.

Chapter 15

The Rest of the Story

Hundreds of passengers, their loved ones, and their families—all suffered, and each died a little on May 12, 2015. Today, some victims are permanently paralyzed. Scores live with pain and physical limitation. Many of us struggle with depression and family issues. Others can no longer hold a job. When you tally the passengers, their spouses, families, friends and careers, it is conceivable that Amtrak 188 changed more than a million lives forever.

My hope is that this book wakes people up and makes them think. Trains are huge responsibilities, yet, in my opinion, the railroad companies are underinsured. Our tracks, tankers, and infrastructure need work. Our antiquated tracks run through high-population areas.

The railroads need to be accountable. Who manages these massive companies? Who is calling the shots? Who do they answer to? Anyone?

Speed controls need to be on all rails everywhere. The southbound side of the tracks at Port Richmond had speed controls on them for years. The northbound side did not. Why not? We don't even know how to get an answer to that question.

I feel strongly that emergency systems and exits on trains need to be revamped ASAP. People need to know how to exit trains. Bigger and better emergency markings and simple signs should be everywhere. Emergency door releases should glow in the dark.

The issue of massive oil tanker trains traveling through cities continues on. A Google search for "bomb train" brings up more and more reports of these explosions.[92] It's time to speak out and take action.

Railroad Policy Changes

As a result of the Amtrak 188 disaster, cameras are now required in the cab of every train.[93]

Automatic Train Control is now on the northbound side of the tracks at Port Richmond.[94]

---

92 https://www.google.com/search?q=bomb+trains&rlz=1C1CHWA
    _enUS633US635&oq=bomb+trains&aqs=chrome.
    0.69i59j69i60l3j35i39j0.2928j0j7&sourceid=chrome&ie=UTF-8
93 https://billypenn.com/2015/07/07/two-months-since-amtrak-188-
    derailed-whats-changed-and-why-big-problems-remain-its-actually-
    cheaper-to-kill-people/
94 Ibid.

In December, 2016, the Federal Railroad Administration made a recommendation that included straightening the sharp curve at the site of the crash.[95]

Government Findings

The National Transportation Safety Board called Amtrak's long failure to implement automatic speed control throughout the busy Northeast Corridor a contributing factor in the crash of Amtrak 188.[96]

Terrorism on the Rails

9/11 had a dress rehearsal, then almost 4,000 people died. The potential for massive deaths is even greater with bomb trains. Keeping quiet didn't work for the airlines. It's not working for the railroads either. In this terrorism environment in which we live, we cannot ignore these warnings. The costs are too great.

Bomb trains are exploding every few weeks and yet no one is raising the alarm. It's time to speak out and take some action. We cannot allow greed to kill our citizens, destroy our property, and wreck our environment.

95 https://www.fws.gov/midwest/endangered/section7/fhwa/pdf/BOwFHWAIbatAndNLEBrevisedDec2016.pdf
96 https://www.ntsb.gov/investigations/AccidentReports/Pages/RAR1602.aspx

Tribute

Looking over the news articles about other passengers was humbling to me. I almost sat in Quiet Car Two. People died in my car, too. At the end of the day, I was lucky. When I feel frustrated at my limitations and I get tired of my pain, I think of my heroes: those who suffer far more than I do, and those who tragically lost their lives.

I am grateful for the support of my friends and my family. I'm thankful for Matisse who tried his best to help me and had patience with my challenges. He saw something in me I did not see in myself. He believed in me and gave me wings to fly. I know we had a once-in-a-lifetime relationship.

Heartfelt thanks to helpful neighbors, firemen and paramedics, law enforcement, and Mayor Michael Nutter who worked throughout the night. And special thanks to my fellow passengers who ignored their own needs to help those of us who were helpless and in the dark.

We are a family.

Afterword

PTSD and depression affect the person inside. No one else can see it, so others are often unaware of its devastation. These conditions affect every relationship the person has, so their family also suffers. I am a voice for many who are depressed or who have had PTSD. Even with all I've learned and how I've grown, my life is not perfect. My wings were damaged in my fall from heaven back to concrete. But I have good friends. One friend with a sense of humor thinks it might be fun to attach a jet engine to the wing of this baby bird. Not only will I fly again. I am going to soar. This is the rebirth of the Phoenix.

They say you can tell a person's character by how they make you feel when you have nothing to offer them. I can say I have been on both sides of that equation. Some who wanted to hang with the best, flattering me and waiting for largesse. Some inspired me. Some became my muses. They helped me finish new projects, dream, invent, and create. But when I lost all due to PTSD and depression, they stepped away.

Some had to let go. Some just felt awkward. Some couldn't deal with me. Some thought I had become beneath them. It happens. Some are takers and others are givers. Life throws us curves. Some curves come with a deadly train.

I don't want anyone else's curve because yours could be far worse than mine.

Clients are forbearing when you bring them value. I was now focusing on business instead of decorating and hosting and putting someone else's needs before my own. I lost me for a moment, but now I'm back. I do business on my own terms. I travel on my own terms, and do what lights me up.

At this moment, I am about five calls from the world's top Executives, and CEOs. I pride myself in my contacts and connections, and I'm a connector on many levels. I have kept every card and every email since the day I started in the recruiting business.

No more looking back. Every day I choose to take baby steps into this new life. It is a brand new season with endless possibilities. Brand new friends. Brand new opportunities. Brand new dreams. So, here I go again. I'm ready for my next amazing adventure. It will be the best one ever. Bring it!

Appendix 1: News Reports

https://www.nytimes.com/interactive/2016/05/17/us/amtrak-train-crash-derailment-philadelphia.html?_r=1

https://mobile.nytimes.com/2016/01/31/magazine/the-wreck-of-amtrak-188.html

https://en.wikipedia.org/wiki/2015_Philadelphia_train_derailment

http://www.philly.com/philly/news/20160202_How_Amtrak_crew_members_and_first_responders_described_the_derailment.html

Appendix 2: Survivors Stories

https://www.brookings.edu/opinions/how-amtrak-failed-the-victims-of-train-188-a-survivors-tale/

http://www.philly.com/philly/news/special_packages/Amtrak_Car_1_survivors_speak_about_their_recovery_a_year_later.html

http://www.ibtimes.com/victims-amtrak-188-disaster-list-names-passengers-who-died-train-derailment-1921359

http://www.abc2news.com/news/in-focus/one-year-later-amtrak-188-survivors-await-final-report-on-cause-of-crash

http://www.philly.com/philly/blogs/in-transit/For-family-of-Amtrak-victims-derailment-an-ordeal-for-them-too.html

https://www.usatoday.com/story/news/2015/11/13/amtrak-crash-survivors-cope-physical-mental-wreckage/75702764/

http://www.latimes.com/nation/la-na-amtrak-witnesses-20150513-story.html

Appendix 3: Fatalities

http://www.nbcnews.com/storyline/amtrak-crash/painful-day-all-eight-fatalities-identified-amtrak-crash-n358306

Appendix 4: Bomb trains

https://news.vice.com/video/bomb-trains-the-crude-gamble-of-oil-by-rail

http://www.thedailybeast.com/derailed-amtrak-cars-nearly-hit-bomb-train

http://www.phillymag.com/citified/2015/05/13/amtrak-crash-oil-tankers/

http://www.phillymag.com/news/2015/02/02/philadelphia-crude-oil-bomb-trains/

Appendix 5: FBI Warns of Terrorism

http://www.thegatewaypundit.com/2015/05/flashback-fbi-warns-of-train-derailment-threat/

Appendix 6: Straightening the curve

http://www.philly.com/philly/business/transportation/Airport-Amtrak-stop-higher-speed-service-recommended-for-Philly-rail.html

About the Author

After surviving the crash of Amtrak 188 on May 12, 2015, Lynn Radice was inspired to write Terror by Rail to show the journey of a survivor lasts far longer than what appears on the nightly news. The passengers of Amtrak 188 boarded the train for a routine ride to New York City, but they got off that train forever changed—in the way they see the world, the way they see their loved ones, and especially the way they see themselves.

Lynn Radice is an expert motivational speaker, career coach, CEO, executive recruiter, thought leader, and job search maven. She is best known for candid self-help job hunting advice and for creating creative job search strategies with her 20 years of corporate, executive, and agency recruiting experience.

Lynn empowers candidates! She has placed top executives and college grads in Poland, Spain, Canada, the UK, Romania and many others. She has traveled to Myanmar, Hong Kong, Thailand, South Africa, France, Switzerland, Spain, and Morocco, speaking with candidates and gathering best practices. She has been published in HR Magazine and hosted a radio show on Voice of America. She's also developing a script for a global awareness movie on dyslexia and the hunt for the Einstein gene.

Lynn Radice is a global advocate of train travel safety. She works tirelessly to build a momentum of change.

Photo Journey

The following is the photo journey of my accident and many train accidents in U.S. and Canada. Please consider signing the petition to get better regulations now. To see these images in color, visit www. TerrorByRail.com.

Emergency personnel work the scene of a train wreck, Tuesday, May 12, 2015, in Philadelphia. An Amtrak train headed to New York City derailed and crashed in Philadelphia. (AP Photo/ Joseph Kaczmarek)

Emergency personnel work the scene of a train wreck, Tuesday, May 12, 2015, in Philadelphia. An Amtrak train headed to New York City derailed and crashed in Philadelphia. (AP Photo/Joseph Kaczmarek)

In this May 13, 2015 photo, emergency personnel work at the scene of a deadly train wreck in Philadelphia. (AP Photo/Patrick Semansky)

A photograph is displayed on a video monitor of the derailment of Amtrak passenger train in Philadelphia last year during a National Transportation Safety Board (NTSB) meeting on the derailment, Tuesday, May 17, 2016, in Washington. (AP Photo/Cliff Owen)

Police and Fire Rescue personnel work the scene of a deadly train wreck, Tuesday, May 12, 2015, in Philadelphia. An Amtrak train headed to New York City derailed and tipped over in Philadelphia on Tuesday night, mangling the front of it, tearing the cars apart and killing several people. (Tom Gralish/The Philadelphia Inquirer via AP)

Investigators examine the train derailment site, Wednesday, May 13, 2015, after a fatal Amtrak derailment Tuesday night, in the Port Richmond section of Philadelphia. Federal investigators arrived Wednesday to determine why an Amtrak train jumped the tracks in a wreck that killed at least six people, and injured dozens. (Alejandro A. Alvarez/Philadelphia Inquirer via AP)

n this aerial photo, emergency personnel work at the scene of a deadly train wreck, Wednesday, May 13, 2015, in Philadelphia. Federal investigators arrived Wednesday to determine why an Amtrak train jumped the tracks in a wreck that killed at least six people, and injured dozens. (AP Photo/Patrick Semansky)

In this aerial photo, emergency personnel work at the scene of a deadly train wreck, Wednesday, May 13, 2015, in Philadelphia. Federal investigators arrived Wednesday to determine why an Amtrak train jumped the tracks in the wreck, Another body has been pulled from the wreckage of an Amtrak train derailment in Philadelphia, increasing the death toll to at least seven. (AP Photo/Patrick Semansky)

Investigators examine the scene of a deadly train wreck, Wednesday, May 13, 2015, in Philadelphia. Federal investigators arrived Wednesday to determine why an Amtrak train jumped the tracks in Tuesday night's fatal accident. (David Swanson (/The Philadelphia Inquirer via AP)

LEFT: The old Lynn, enjoying life in style in Europe. RIGHT:In Hong Kong.

Fearless and free before the accident.

LEFT: Taken at the hospital, deep bruising on my arm. CENTER: My remaining shoe and sooty jeans from the accident. RIGHT: My lady toupee.

Smoke rises from railway cars that were carrying crude oil after derailing in downtown Lac Megantic, Que., Saturday, July 6, 2013. A large swath of Lac Megantic was destroyed Saturday after a train carrying crude oil derailed, sparking several explosions and forcing the evacuation of up to 1,000 people. (AP Photo/The Canadian Press, Paul Chiasson)

In this June 19, 2009 file photo, a car at right is seen engulfed in flames from rail cars loaded with ethanol that derailed in Rockford, Ill. A Rockford woman died as she tried to flee the derailment. Environmental groups asked the U.S. Department of Transportation to immediately ban shipments of volatile crude oil in older railroad tank cars, citing oil train wrecks and explosions and the agency's own findings that accidents pose an imminent hazard. The petition filed Tuesday, July 15, 2014, by the Sierra Club and ForestEthics seeks an emergency order within 30 days to prohibit crude oil from the Bakken region of the Northern Plains and elsewhere from being carried in the older tank cars, known as DOT-111s. (AP Photo/Rockford Register Star, Scott Morgan, File)

Smoke and flames erupt from the scene of a train derailment Thursday, March 5, 2015, near Galena, Ill. A BNSF Railway freight train loaded with crude oil derailed around 1:20 p.m. in a rural area where the Galena River meets the Mississippi, said Jo Daviess County Sheriff's Sgt. Mike Moser. (AP Photo/Telegraph Herald, Mike Burley)

Derailed oil tanker train cars burn near Mount Carbon, W.Va., Monday, Feb. 16, 2015. A CSX train carrying more than 100 tankers of crude oil derailed in a snowstorm, sending a fireball into the sky and threatening the water supply of nearby residents, authorities and residents said Tuesday. (AP Photo/The Daily Mail, Marcus Constantino)

In this Dec. 30, 2013, file photo, a fireball goes up at the site of an oil train derailment in Casselton, N.D. State Environmental Health Chief Dave Glatt says cleanup after the BNSF train derailed and caught fire in the small southeastern North Dakota town "is all but complete." Federal investigators determined that 400,000 gallons of oil was lost in the derailment. (AP Photo/Bruce Crummy, File)

Train tank cars with placards indicating petroleum crude oil stand idle on the tracks in Philadelphia Wednesday, Aug. 26, 2015. While railroads have long carried hazardous materials through congested urban areas, cities are now scrambling to formulate emergency plans and to train firefighters amid the latest safety threat: a fiftyfold increase in crude shipments that critics say has put millions of people living or working near the tracks at heightened risk of derailment, fire and explosion. (AP Photo/Matt Rourke)

A man walks past homes, condominiums, and train tank cars with signs indicating petroleum crude oil standing idle on the tracks in Philadelphia on Wednesday, Aug. 26, 2015. Activists in Philadelphia question whether the city has adequately communicated its evacuation plans with residents who would have to leave quickly after an accident. (AP Photo/Matt Rourke)

In this photo taken April 9, 2015, a man walks his dog past train tank cars with placards indicating petroleum crude oil standing idle on the tracks, in Philadelphia. Rail tank cars that are used to transport most crude oil and many other flammable liquids will have to be built to stronger standards to reduce the risk of catastrophic train crash and fire under a series of new rules unveiled Friday by U.S. and Canadian transportation officials. (AP Photo/Matt Rourke)

Please join us at www.TerrorByRail.com and on social media. Be sure to sign the petition at www.TerrorByRail.com as well. Together we can make a difference.

Twitter: https://twitter.com/terrorbyrail
Facebook: www.facebook.com/terrorbyrail
Instagram: https://www.instagram.com/terrorbyrail/
Pinterest: https://www.pinterest.com/terrorbyrail/
LinkedIn: https://www.linkedin.com/company/11258362/

Morgan James
Speakers Group

www.TheMorganJamesSpeakersGroup.com

We connect Morgan James published
authors with live and online events
and audiences who will benefit
from their expertise.